HOW TO SAY IT

Persuasive Presentations

Dale —
Always make an
impact! *Dale*

Jeffrey Jacobi

PRENTICE HALL PRESS

PRENTICE HALL PRESS
Published by the Penguin Group
Penguin Group (USA) Inc.
375 Hudson Street, New York, New York 10014, USA
Penguin Group (Canada), 90 Eglinton Avenue East, Suite 700, Toronto, Ontario M4P 2Y3, Canada
(a division of Pearson Penguin Canada Inc.)
Penguin Books Ltd., 80 Strand, London WC2R 0RL, England
Penguin Group Ireland, 25 St. Stephen's Green, Dublin 2, Ireland (a division of Penguin Books Ltd.)
Penguin Group (Australia), 250 Camberwell Road, Camberwell, Victoria 3124, Australia
(a division of Pearson Australia Group Pty. Ltd.)
Penguin Books India Pvt. Ltd., 11 Community Centre, Panchsheel Park, New Delhi—110 017, India
Penguin Group (NZ), Cnr. Airborne and Rosedale Roads, Albany, Auckland 1310, New Zealand
(a division of Pearson New Zealand Ltd.)
Penguin Books (South Africa) (Pty.) Ltd., 24 Sturdee Avenue, Rosebank, Johannesburg 2196,
South Africa

Penguin Books Ltd., Registered Offices: 80 Strand, London WC2R 0RL, England

While the author has made every effort to provide accurate telephone numbers and Internet addresses at
the time of publication, neither the publisher nor the author assumes any responsibility for errors, or for
changes that occur after publication. Further, publisher does not have any control over and does not assume any responsibility for author or third-party websites or their content.

First edition: October 2006

Library of Congress Cataloging-in-Publication Data

Jacobi, Jeffrey.
    How to say it : persuasive presentations / Jeff Jacobi.
       p.   cm.
    Includes index.
    ISBN 0-7352-0411-X
1. Business presentations.   2. Public speaking.   I. Title.
    HF5718.22.J33 2006
    658.4'52—dc22

                                                       2006014745

PRINTED IN THE UNITED STATES OF AMERICA

10 9 8 7 6 5 4 3

Most Prentice Hall books are available at special quantity discounts for bulk purchases for sales
promotions, premiums, fund-raising, or educational use. Special books, or book excerpts, can also be
created to fit specific needs. For details, write: Special Markets, The Berkley Publishing Group, 375
Hudson Street, New York, New York 10014.

Acknowledgments

My heartfelt thanks to my wife, Rosemary, for her unwavering support, patience, and wonderful sense of humor. To my son, Michael, and my mother, Tanya, with love and affection.

Special thanks to Christel Winkler, Jeff McCartney, Mark Misercola, and Michel LeGall, for their help and guidance.

Contents

Introduction

Giving a speech or a presentation isn't something most people would readily volunteer for. In fact, in poll after poll, most people say they fear giving a speech more than dying. Even the pros who do this every day say they feel the anxiety. Yet it doesn't have to be that way. Working with *How to Say It: Persuasive Presentations* requires a fine blend of patience, practice, and perseverance. If you're willing to make the investment up front, by reading this book and practicing what it preaches, then you can expect to reap the rewards.

As the title suggests, this is a book about becoming a powerful and persuasive presenter. And I'm not just talking about formal business presentations. I'm talking about presenting yourself in typical, everyday situations at the office and in your community. From client presentations to PTA meetings, your ideas and your reputation will be stronger and more compelling if you know how to say it with a persuasive presentation.

But making a powerful presentation requires a much broader set of skills than most people realize. It certainly involves more than just preparing the "right materials."

Presentation skills are not just about making the "big presentation." They're about how you present yourself in a variety of situations. When most of us hear the word "presentation," our minds naturally turn to the mechanics of creating pitch books and PowerPoint slides or the long process of writing a formal speech.

But that's just one small slice of the presentation picture. The reality is we use our presentation skills all the time— whether we're conscious of it or not—the moment we meet a client, colleague, or neighbor. The way we speak and share our thoughts and selves with others are what presentation skills are all about—regardless of the setting. Voice mails, conference calls, one-on-one interactions, and roundtable discussions are all presentations.

As a presentation coach for more than two decades, I've had the opportunity and privilege to work with a wide variety of clients, from actors to actuaries. I've listened to and observed hundreds of presentations in many different venues from business to politics and from law to the media. From my perspective, there are two basic types of speakers. The first are those who recite the facts in a disconnected way, unaware of their audience. The second are those who engage the audience by inviting them to listen to and remember a clear and compelling message.

In today's hypercompetitive business environment, it's not enough to be intelligent or to command the big business issues. Strong problem-solving abilities and powerful analytical skills alone don't guarantee you'll be successful. I've seen the careers of too many talented, promising, and motivated professionals derailed by poor presentation skills. And I've seen many first-rate proposals and business ideas die a painful death because of dull and disorganized presentations.

On the flip side, I've seen the careers of those who are able to communicate with clarity and impact really take off. When these people speak they take command of the room and the attention of their audiences. With a steady hand and voice, they guide their listeners; they captivate their audiences, and take them where they want.

The fact is most audiences can't distinguish between the messenger and the message. What your listeners think about you as a person, and the image you project, will directly affect their evaluation of your ideas, your professionalism, and your ability to make a positive difference for them.

Like it or not, people are ultimately judged not by what they know or do, but by the way they present themselves. Nothing you can do for your career will give you as much of a boost as improving your presentation skills. And that's the idea behind *How to Say It: Persuasive Presentations*. Here you'll find handy "How to Say It" and "How Not to Say It" recaps at the end of each chapter. These serve as the perfect refreshers on the way to (or just before) a presentation. You'll be able to dive into this book at any point and immediately learn to use a proven tip or technique. In the time it takes to commute to work you can master the skills that are necessary to become an effective and dynamic presenter.

1

Confidence and Poise Under Pressure

"All the world's a stage. And all the men and women merely players." If Shakespeare was right and all the world is a stage, can you afford to have stage fright?

Would you turn down a promotion because the new position required public speaking? I know people who have.

A little nervousness can be good for you. Even the most experienced speakers, actors, and athletes get anxious before they perform. Which is okay—a certain amount of nervous energy can actually give you that extra edge and focused concentration to reach your peak level of performance. The challenge is to channel your fear of speaking into a positive outcome—to make it a friend, not a foe. When it comes to presenting (and with apologies to Franklin Roosevelt) we really have nothing to fear but fear itself. Let's take the fear out of the process and put the confidence in one step at a time, starting with a brief self-assessment.

The worksheet here will help you evaluate your presentation skills. It's designed to increase your awareness of important presentation issues and identify some of your inherent strengths and challenges as a presenter.

Answer the statements in the worksheet as honestly as you can. Put a check mark by the appropriate response.

1. It is hard for me to present with confidence in high-pressure situations.

____ Most of the time ____ Frequently ____ Occasionally ____ Almost never

2. When delivering a talk, I prefer speaking from a full text rather than using a bullet-point outline.

____ Most of the time ____ Frequently ____ Occasionally ____ Almost never

3. People tell me I talk too fast.

____ Most of the time ____ Frequently ____ Occasionally ____ Almost never

4. I feel more comfortable when interacting with others during a presentation than I do when delivering uninterrupted remarks.

____ Most of the time ____ Frequently ____ Occasionally ____ Almost never

5. I spend most of my time preparing the content of a talk and considerably less time focusing on the delivery.

____ Most of the time ____ Frequently ____ Occasionally ____ Almost never

6. I sense that people have a hard time understanding me.

____ Most of the time ____ Frequently ____ Occasionally ____ Almost never

7. I have a hard time grabbing and holding my listeners' attention.

____ Most of the time ____ Frequently ____ Occasionally ____ Almost never

8. I sound like I'm reading when I speak from a prepared text.

___ Most of the time ___ Frequently ___ Occasionally ___ Almost never

9. I'm unsure of how I present myself to others.

___ Most of the time ___ Frequently ___ Occasionally ___ Almost never

10. I go beyond my allotted time limit when making a presentation.

___ Most of the time ___ Frequently ___ Occasionally ___ Almost never

11. I worry about how I'll sound before I begin a meeting or presentation.

___ Most of the time ___ Frequently ___ Occasionally ___ Almost never

12. I feel uncomfortable when I am suddenly called upon to speak.

___ Most of the time ___ Frequently ___ Occasionally ___ Almost never

13. I experience shortness of breath when speaking before large groups.

___ Most of the time ___ Frequently ___ Occasionally ___ Almost never

14. I salt my speech with fillers such as "like," "you know," "uh," "okay," etc.

___ Most of the time ___ Frequently ___ Occasionally ___ Almost never

15. I don't have a systematic approach to prepare and rehearse for my presentations.

___ Most of the time ___ Frequently ___ Occasionally ___ Almost never

16. I think more about *what* I'm going to say than *how* I'm going to say it.

____ Most of the time ____ Frequently ____ Occasionally ____ Almost never

17. It is difficult for me to convey complex ideas in a clear, concise manner.

____ Most of the time ____ Frequently ____ Occasionally ____ Almost never

18. It's hard for me to express myself naturally when speaking before large groups.

____ Most of the time ____ Frequently ____ Occasionally ____ Almost never

19. I don't think about the nonverbal signals I am sending.

____ Most of the time ____ Frequently ____ Occasionally ____ Almost never

20. I have a hard time getting my point across in a fast-paced meeting when there's no break in the discussion.

____ Most of the time ____ Frequently ____ Occasionally ____ Almost never

Now look at the statements where you checked off "most of the time" or "frequently." These are the areas you want to focus on in particular as you work with this book and the advice in each chapter.

Regardless of which areas you identify as your own challenges, every problem listed in the worksheet will improve if you embrace two concepts fully: preparation and practice. This is true even where the difficulties seem to stem directly from excess anxiety. But what makes us so anxious about presenting? The short answer is many of us become anxious because we're afraid of being embarrassed.

After all, who wants to look foolish in front of others? Not to mention all that's riding on the outcome. If things don't go well it could raise doubts about your competence and reputation. The mere thought of having six hundred—or just six—eyes glued to your every word can be very intimidating. But the truth is neither anxiety nor pressure is the real problem here. I'm convinced the real culprit lies in a lack of adequate preparation. It holds true regardless of whether you're preparing for a formal presentation or just gathering some thoughts before being pulled into an unexpected meeting.

In many cases, time (or more specifically the lack of it) frequently limits what you can do to prepare. But I'm going to let you in on a little secret. You don't need to devote a ton of time to preparation. The real key is to find the right preparation approach for whatever time you have, whether it's a full set of notes or a single note card with four or five trigger words to jog your memory. Once you've settled on an approach, it's just as important to follow through. For many this is the biggest challenge—as difficult as giving the presentation itself. In fact, many of the clients I've counseled tell me they actually do better—much better—when they're well prepared. But the real irony is they're almost always reluctant to practice!

I've heard all the excuses, too, everything from "I'm just too busy" to "I'll read through it several times on the plane" to "I was making last-minute changes late into the night and couldn't get around to it." Unless this is a presentation you've given hundreds of times, procrastination simply doesn't cut it.

Preparation is not about time—it's about discipline. Like

watching what you eat, exercising, paying the bills, and do-ing household chores, preparing and practicing is not always pleasant. But think about what happens when you simply let things take their course. Eventually, lack of preparation be-comes a self-defeating habit. The more you stumble, the more nervous you get. The more nervous you become, the more it shows when you're presenting. It's a vicious circle.

So what can you do about it? Read on.

PLAN, PREPARE, AND PRACTICE TO BUILD CONFIDENCE

Good preparation is a concrete process with specific steps—not just a mind game to psych yourself up. Accord-ing to a recent article published in the *Guardian*, Apple Computer CEO Steve Jobs and his team put in weeks of in-tensive preparation for his major presentations. Jobs follows a series of precise steps to get every detail just right. Once the planning and preparing stages are completed, he typi-cally rehearses two days in advance of his talk. He does sev-eral run-throughs in front of a live audience (the product and engineering managers) and asks for their feedback as well. The hard work and preparation really show. If you've ever watched a webcast of a Mac product launch, it is bril-liantly crafted and truly spectacular, with Steve Jobs giving a memorable performance.

Step One: Plan Ahead

Start ahead of time, even if you don't have all the details in place. Familiarize yourself with the five "Knows" of prepa-ration coming up in chapter 2:

1. Know your purpose.
2. Know your audience.
3. Know your approach.
4. Know your material.
5. Know your speaking environment.

Know them all and you're well on the way to knowing what it takes to successfully prepare for your presentation.

Step Two: Prepare the Message

Determine the key take-aways you want your audience to remember. Structure your thoughts so the flow of ideas will be crystal clear to your audience. Add anecdotes, analogies, and examples to illustrate your points, especially when referring to statistics. For example, if you say "our sales increased 120 percent," add: "or put another way, we sold more hot dogs in the past twelve months than we did in the previous twelve years." Create a strong opening that captures your audience's attention. Likewise, you'll want to close on a strong, memorable note that reiterates your point of view. More on this in chapter 3.

Step Three: Practice!

Practicing or rehearsing is by far the weakest link in the preparation process, so although it is the third "step," it is the first thing we must focus on here. Most business professionals don't know how important rehearsing is and they don't know how to properly rehearse. In fact, 90 percent or more of preparation time is typically devoted to content. Countless hours go into creating and fine-tuning the presentation materials, and whatever time is left over—if there is any time left over—is reserved for practice. Yet how you practice can literally make or break your presentation. Keep in mind that great presentations often die on the vine because they aren't rehearsed properly, or they're never rehearsed at all. If you're like many people, you probably don't have a lot of lead time to prepare. But the good news, as noted earlier, is that in most cases efficient practice doesn't require a major time commitment.

The simple techniques described below won't take a lot of time, but they will ensure your presentation is a genuine success.

REHEARSAL TECHNIQUES THAT REALLY WORK

Practice Out Loud

The only way to get truly comfortable and confident with your material is to try it out. Reading it silently to yourself isn't the same as practicing your presentation aloud. There's a big difference. Practicing aloud gives you a real sense of how the words sound and, equally important, how *you* sound. Keep in mind that what you've written won't always go over well when spoken. The more complex the language, the harder it is to convey. So it's important to make sure everything you've written is easy to say. Use words that are easy to pronounce. Keep it simple when you speak. Avoid jargon and fancy "MBA-speak." Instead, aim for short, punchy sentences. Edit for ease of delivery. Then work the kinks out by practicing aloud. Practice with a tape recorder so you can play back your presentation and actually hear how you sound. Listen for content as well as delivery. Monitor your voice inflection, pace, and clarity of pronunciation. What else can you do?

- Practice with a video camera so you can actually see and hear how you're coming across. Take a look at your posture, gestures, facial expressions, and eye contact. How heavily are you relying on your notes?
- Practice in front of a mirror. If you're in a hotel room and don't have access to a tape recorder or video camera, this is a good way to see and hear yourself.
- Practice in front of friends, family, or colleagues. There's no substitute for a live audience. If you really want to gain confidence and poise under pressure, you have to practice speaking in front of people.

Simulate the Conditions of Your Speaking Environment

If your presentation calls for a pitch book or PowerPoint, make sure you practice with it. Test your computer ahead of time so that everything is running smoothly. If you're doing a roundtable presentation, sit at a table when you practice or, better yet, get a conference room to practice in. If you're delivering a speech from a podium, create a makeshift podium by placing a box on top of a table to rest your notes on. The bottom line: Do whatever you can to create a realistic simulation. Additional ideas:

- Dress for the occasion. Put on the same shirt, suit, or dress you'll wear for the event when you practice. If you think you're overdoing it, ask yourself just how much is at stake.
- Make friends with the room. If possible, try to practice in the room where your presentation will take place. For big presentations, contact the event organizer to get access to the space beforehand.

Why go to these lengths? Having a practice ritual exposes your strengths and weaknesses in advance, and allows you to make corrections before you speak. When the time comes to face your audience, you'll be spared the high anxiety and stage fright that many unprepared speakers experience, and you'll enjoy the comfort and confidence that comes from being well rehearsed.

Seek Out Opportunities to Speak in Low-Risk Situations

If you belong to a religious organization, volunteer to speak at your house of worship. Join committees at your workplace and practice by speaking out on important issues. Look for opportunities to speak in your community. Some possibilities may include your tenant association, your Parent-Teacher Association, or fraternal clubs. Even proposing a toast at a dinner party is a good start. The more you speak in public, the easier it gets. Who knows, you might even start to enjoy it after a while.

Don't Let Them See You Sweat

A dry mouth, rapid heartbeat, shortness of breath, shaky voice, and trembling hands and knees—sound familiar? If you experience any of these symptoms in front of an audience, don't panic. Here are some simple techniques you can use to help regain control.

Relax Those Tight Muscles

When you get nervous, your mouth, throat, and jaw tighten up. A tight throat can disrupt your air flow and cause shallow breathing. This can make your voice sound weak and thin, which in turn leads to quivering. The silent breathing exercise below will relax your mouth, throat, and jaw and help you achieve better breath control.

1. Using the breath only, without speaking aloud, exhale on the syllable PAH-H-H-H-H-H-H-H-H-H-H-H.
   a. Aim for a long, even-flowing stream of air.
   b. Breathe normally.
   c. Open your mouth wide and keep the mouth, throat, and jaw relaxed. (Think of the mouth position you use when the doctor examines your throat.)
   d. Repeat: PAH-H-H-H-H-H-H-H-H-H-H-H.
2. Now slowly exhale on TAH-H-H-H-H-H-H-H-H-H-H.
3. Now slowly exhale on KAH-H-H-H-H-H-H-H-H-H-H.
4. Finally, slowly exhale on MAH-H-H-H-H-H-H-H-H.

These easy breathing techniques are excellent stress reducers, and because they're silent they can be done just about anywhere without disturbing anyone. Doing a series of these before you speak can really calm your nerves and alleviate those last-minute jitters.

Control Those Trembling Hands and Knees

Using big, broad gestures as you speak helps release excess tension from your body, and it will do wonders for trembling hands. This is true whether you're doing a stand-up presentation or you're seated at a conference table. If your knees are shaking and you're not behind a podium, move around a bit. Don't be a stiff! For more on gestures and movement, see chapter 9.

Concentrate on the Job at Hand— Stay Focused

If you worry about what others are thinking of you, you won't be focused on your job. This is not the time to be self-conscious. After all, you can't be a critic and performer at the same time. Try to channel your energy and emotions into your material. Get involved in what you are saying. And keep in mind that in most cases your audience really does want you to succeed. Many people become preoccupied and flustered when speaking before a group and suffer lapses in their concentration. What can you do about this?

Create a distraction to test your level of concentration:

- Practice your presentation with the TV or radio on.
- Run through a portion of your presentation with a kitchen timer set for three minutes. When it rings, think of a client asking a specific question and then answer it. See how quickly you can regain your original thought or transition to your next point. Reset the timer and repeat this process several times.
- Do part of your talk closing one eye or standing on one leg. Then try closing one eye *and* standing on one leg simultaneously.
- Sing the words to your presentation. That's right, make a song out of it.

Sound ridiculous? Don't worry, there's a method to this madness. If you can get through your presentation with all these distractions, speaking normally in front of a group will be a piece of cake!

Practice out of Order to Stay on Track

Mix things up a bit. Start at different points in your presentation. For example, open with section two, three, or four. Begin in the middle of a section. Practice out of sequence; jump around from section to section. While I was a student at the Juilliard School, my teacher once had me play a concerto out of order. He would stop periodically and make me restart in the middle of another section. At first, this was all very confusing and distracting, but I soon came to realize that it served an important purpose. It quickly exposed just how well I knew the piece. When presenting, most people only practice in a linear order from start to finish, which means they know their content in order of sequence. Consequently, they're more prone to lose their place when a client or colleague interrupts with a question that takes them off-point. They often "freeze" for a moment and have a hard time getting back on track. Practicing out of order allows you to maintain a clear focus and get back on message no matter where you are in your remarks. It's a great way to deal with any unexpected interruptions during your actual presentation. It's also a great technique to help you manage more informal meetings or presentations when you wind up having to jump around a bit.

Pace Yourself to Stay in Control

When we're nervous we tend to speak too fast. The opening of a presentation is typically when your anxiety level is highest. Your body is charged up with a healthy dose of adrenaline, and the result is that you often rush through your material. A bad case of nerves can distort your sense of timing and make you unaware of your own speed. What feels like a normal pace to you may be way too fast for your audience. So make a point of starting out slowly and deliberately, and remember to pause to breathe as you speak. This will help you stay in control. Remember, confident speakers don't rush.

Start Out Big and Strong

Don't be a mouse, be a lion! Don't walk, or speak, on eggshells. If you're nervous your voice will sound timid and tentative. Speak up! Project your voice to help prevent cracking or quivering. Your voice and breathing need a few moments to synchronize. It's better to start out with short sentences to get the power in your voice. For example, in one breath say, "Good morning." (Pause for a breath) "I'm really excited to be here today." (Pause) Saying fewer words in each breath at the start of your presentation will give you better voice control and get your words out with greater confidence and conviction.

Know Your First Sixty Seconds
Without Notes

The first sixty seconds of your presentation is perhaps the most critical part of your presentation. It's where you establish your credibility and credentials. It's where you either grab your audience or lose them. And it comes at a critical point when listeners are forming opinions about you. Your job is to demonstrate that you're worthy of your listeners' time and attention even before the presentation begins. Yet despite its importance, the first sixty seconds is frequently the most nonpracticed piece of the presentation. Don't fall into this trap. Rehearse your opening until you know it cold. You should be able to deliver the first sixty seconds of your remarks while maintaining eye contact with your audience without looking down at your notes. Not only will this make your audience comfortable, it will speak volumes about your confidence.

HOW TO SAY IT

1. Realize that it's okay to feel a little nervous, but know you are in control of it.
2. Allow ample time to prepare.
3. Develop a practice ritual.
4. Practice aloud—preferably with audio or videotape or in front of people.
5. Simulate the conditions of your speaking environment.
6. Calm your nerves with proven breathing techniques.
7. Use big, broad gestures to release nervous tension from your body.
8. Stay focused on your job at hand.
9. Pace yourself by speaking deliberately.
10. Start with a strong voice and short sentences to prevent quivering.
11. Know your first sixty seconds without notes.

HOW NOT TO SAY IT

1. Don't avoid speaking in public just because you don't like it.
2. Don't procrastinate in preparing.
3. Don't give yourself a false sense of confidence by

minimizing the importance of your presentation. (Ah . . . it's no big deal!)

4. Don't just wing it—this is a hit-or-miss strategy and you will miss more than you hit.
5. Don't just read to yourself—that's not practicing.
6. Don't worry about what others may be thinking of you.
7. Don't feel physically constrained.
8. Don't speak too fast—don't look and sound like you want it to be over soon.
9. Don't rely heavily on your notes during the opening of the presentation.
10. Don't forget to breathe.

2

Prepare for the Unexpected

You're on tap to present. It's a given. So what do you do first? Before beginning any presentation or meeting there are some things you need to know. Specifically, you need to know five fundamental points that underlie the success of any presentation.

The Five "Knows"
1. Know your purpose.
2. Know your audience.
3. Know your approach.
4. Know your material.
5. Know your speaking environment.

1. Know Your Purpose

Why is it so important for your presentation to have a clear purpose? For starters, the purpose affects your mindset, how you think about your presentation, how you deliver it, and, ultimately, how it is received. Keep in mind, the purpose of your presentation isn't the same as the subject. The purpose is the "why" behind the words: the aim, goal, or objective of your presentation. It's the main reason why you're giving the presentation; it states your *intentions*.

To be a convincing presenter you must have a compelling purpose, something that interests and excites you. Most importantly, your purpose must be *actionable*. By that, I mean it has to make you and your audience want to do something or make something happen. It should energize and excite you. Because if you don't feel strongly about what you're saying, there's no way you'll be able to excite your audience and move them to action.

To find an actionable purpose, begin by asking yourself the following questions:

- What is the reason I am giving this presentation?
- What results or outcome do I want?

Typically when I ask people to state their purpose or intention, they say things like, "I want to *update, inform, explain, tell,*" etc. These are not *energizing* intentions. They're really *informative* intentions. Think about the difference. You can "tell" or "explain" a strategy to your audience or you can "excite" your audience about your strategy. Which purpose or intention do you think will help you speak with more conviction? The bottom line: Don't settle for a vague or low-conviction purpose. You need an action that will get your juices going. If, for example, you're giving an update, dig a bit deeper and ask yourself, What is the specific reason for the update? What are you trying to accomplish? Do you want to motivate, persuade, ingratiate, reassure, warn, or challenge? These are compelling actions. They will ultimately engage your audience because they have engaged you first. Always aim for a compelling purpose. So if you're making a presentation to inform analysts about the prospects for your company's stock, wouldn't it be better to do more than just inform them? Give them some reasons why management at your company is excited about your firm's prospects—tell them why you believe your company is going to grow and say it with conviction.

Sometimes a presentation can have more than one purpose. Just as scenes in a theatrical performance have different intentions or actions to support the overall story, your presentation may require different intentions to support your main objective. I typically ask clients to identify the specific intentions in each section of their presentation. Most people are not accustomed to this level of analysis, but the payoff is significant. The deeper they dig, the more committed they sound.

This is what makes former president Bill Clinton such a memorable speaker. He understands every specific intention in every section of his talk, and can effectively communicate each intention to support his main objective.

Once you've determined what the right intention is, it's important to match your delivery or tone with your intention. For example, clients will often say they want to "excite" their audience but when they start speaking they don't look or sound the least bit excited. (You'll find more on effective delivery techniques in chapters 8 and 9.)

2. Know Your Audience

A common mistake many presenters make is preparing their presentation without the audience in mind. This is the equivalent of going sailing without checking the weather.

You can avoid a lot of rough weather by asking the following questions about your audience:

1. What's their background? Are they all from the same or different backgrounds in terms of rank, experience, expertise, culture, and education? Are you speaking to investment bankers, management consultants, loan officers, accountants, lawyers, insurance executives, restaurant owners, or a mix?

2. How well do they understand your subject? Be careful not to talk over the heads of your audience. A vice president at a major bank complained that her manager had a habit of getting way too technical about his topic during client meetings. Clients couldn't grasp what he was saying and would frequently leave meetings confused and frustrated.

   How exactly do you determine your audience's knowledge level? Do some research. Go to colleagues at your company and ask them what they know about the people you'll be speaking to. Get right to the point: "My subject is XYZ—how technical can I be? What is their level of understanding of the topic and issues at hand? Are they highly sophisticated, or do they just have a general knowledge about the subject?" If you're presenting to a small group, try to find out about the dynamics of the group. What are the personalities of the people? Are they highly analytical or highly assertive? Are they friendly and easygoing or fast-paced and action-oriented? Different personality styles may require different approaches.

If you can't find out much about your audience ahead of time, here are a few techniques you can use during the presentation:

a. Poll the group at the start to determine their knowledge level. For example, ask: "What are your thoughts on the current hedging strategy?" "What has been your experience with the new tax initiative?" Based on how they answer a few targeted questions and the terminology they use, you'll get a pretty good sense of what they know and don't know.

b. Encourage them to ask questions along the way. Tell your audience at the outset that you want an interactive dialogue. It's perfectly okay to say something like, "Please feel free to stop me if you don't understand something I've said, or if you would like me to clarify anything." You can also ask them to let you know if they're already familiar with a particular area you're discussing so you can avoid covering old ground.

c. Periodically ask questions to solicit feedback and clarify their understanding. The more complex and technical the subject matter, the more you should stop and recap along the way to make sure everyone is on the same page.

d. Be on the lookout for verbal and nonverbal cues. If your listeners look dazed, bored, or confused, you probably need to change your approach. How do you handle audiences with varying degrees of knowledge? One of the best ways is to call on the higher-knowledge folks and ask them to share their experiences with the group. Give them a little leeway to impart their knowledge. Have them cofacilitate—they will love you for it! If you're not sure how familiar your audience is with your topic, it's always safer to err on the cautious side and assume they know less than more. It's easier and less embarrassing for your audience to ask for a higher level of discussion than to ask you to "dumb it down." Also, keep in mind that many people would rather sit quietly and take in nothing than risk losing face in front of their colleagues by admitting they don't understand what you're talking about.

3. What preconceived notions might the audience have about your topic, your company, or you as a professional? What is their history with your organization? Have they had a bad experience with your company in the past? Knowing the answer to these questions will help you determine how direct, subtle, forthright, or guarded you might need to be. Are there some in the audience who would be skeptical or strongly disagree with your message? What if there is a hot-button issue—how sensitive do you need to be?

4. What do you want your audience to think or do at the end of your presentation? Do you want them to think differently about an issue? Are you trying to get them to take some kind of action? This is a good place to begin your thought process.

3. Know Your Approach

The type of presentation you give is critical. You will want to find the right style and tone for the occasion. So you need to ask yourself: "Do I want to have a casual conversation or a more formal presentation? Do I want the meeting to be highly interactive, exchanging opinions and ideas throughout my presentation? Or will I deliver uninterrupted, prepared remarks and take questions at the end?" No one can answer these for you. If you want more give-and-take, be sure to ask plenty of questions up front and listen attentively to the responses. Your audience needs to really believe you're interested in their participation.

Whatever you do, be flexible in your approach. You may go into a meeting expecting to give more of a formal, "by-the-book" presentation, only to find out your client wants an informal dialogue. If you're not prepared for this, you could stumble badly.

In terms of personal style, consider the kind of image you want to project. Do you want to appear presidential, or do you want to be more approachable and come across as "one of them"? There is a significant difference in how others perceive you if you walk into the audience or remain behind a podium.

Will you be presenting as part of a team? If you're part of a group presentation, will you be leading the discussion or playing a supporting role, interjecting your thoughts occasionally along the way? If you're leading the presentation, will you be doing most of the talking or will you be more of a moderator; facilitating the discussion as other team members present different sections? Who will be speaking before and after you and what approach should you take to complement the different speaking styles? If you're playing a supporting role, how assertive do you need to be to get your points across?

4. Know Your Material

Are you qualified to give the presentation? Make sure you
know what you're talking about. A partner-led team at a
leading management consulting firm once lost out on a
major project simply because they didn't have the knowledge and expertise in the room to answer a key question
from the CEO they were pitching to. They spent countless
hours preparing and fine-tuning the presentation book but
were unable to support key pieces of information con-
tained in their presentation.

Put your knowledge to the test. Have a colleague or
two play devil's advocate. Encourage them to challenge
you and shoot holes in your logic. Chances are if you can
pass this test, you can pass muster with the CEO. Another
way to test your knowledge is to do a test run without
notes or visuals. If you can make it through without awkward gaps in your thought process, you should be in
good shape. At the very least, you should be able to hit
the main points or ideas in a logical sequence without any
notes.

So what happens if you're not an expert but are asked to
present anyway? Sometimes you can't decline. Perhaps
your manager has a pressing commitment and needs you
to fill in. Here are a few steps to get up to speed:

- Don't apologize to your audience for not being well
  prepared.
- Gather information, ideas, and opinions from colleagues.
- Get coached through the material. Don't just read it
  through; seek out the perspectives of others.

- Consider taking on more of a facilitator role. Actively involve your audience and encourage an exchange of ideas. Get them to share their thoughts and experiences. Draw upon their knowledge and expertise.

5. Know Your Speaking Environment

Knowing the lay of the land is important because where you speak can influence how you speak. For example, a PR executive recently gave a talk to over 150 marketing professionals. He was a little bent out of shape when he arrived the morning of the conference because he was caught off guard by the layout of the space. Not liking podiums, he wanted to walk around as he spoke. But the space was so restricted and crammed with chairs, there was literally no room for him to move. His only choice was to speak behind a podium tucked away in the corner. He made do, but had he known about the speaking environment in advance he would have prepared differently.

You can eliminate surprises by asking a few simple questions:

- What's the size of the space?
- Is there a raised platform or stage? If so, how big is it?
- What's the shape of the room? Is it wider than it is long? Are there columns?
- How are the seats arranged? Is it tiered theater style, banquet style, or straight rows? Are the chairs arranged in a semicircle or U-shape? Can you walk into the audience? Some of this can be altered if you ask ahead of time.
- If you are speaking at a large conference, can you get a diagram of the space in advance? This will enable you

to get a firsthand look at the room layout. Try to visualize the space before you actually see it. Ideally, try to
rehearse in the room beforehand to "make friends
with the room." It really helps.

- Will you be using a podium or walking around? What
  type of microphone will you use, a podium mike or
  clip-on, or both?

- What's the lighting like? If your talk is being video-
  taped, make sure there are no spotlights shining
  directly into your eyes. Also, the room lights should always be bright enough so you can see the eyes of your
  audience.

- Is there a place nearby for a glass of water? (Always
  use a glass. Don't swig from a cheap plastic water bot-
  tle. And avoid ice water; drink room temperature water instead.)

- Who's changing the slides—you or someone else?
  Does the technical staff have a script that indicates the
  slide changes? Request a run-through so they know
  what to do.

- Will you be using a teleprompter or floor monitor?
  Technical glitches happen, so always, *always* have a
  hard copy of your presentation nearby.

- Is there a rehearsal room or space where you can col-
  lect your thoughts ahead of time?

HOW TO SAY IT

1. Find a compelling purpose that can drive you to be
   your best.
2. Analyze your presentation to determine if there is
   more than one purpose.

3. Make sure you can effectively communicate your purpose or intention as you transition from one section to another.
4. Know your audience like you know yourself.
5. Poll your audience in some way to determine their knowledge level.
6. Be flexible enough to change formats and styles on short notice.
7. Think about the image you want to project.
8. Always prepare for the unexpected issue or angle, especially on a controversial subject.
9. Test how well you know your talk by practicing the main points of your presentation out loud without notes.
10. Test your environment—room plan, sound, and lights—so you'll be ready for action.
11. Make sure the technical crew have the information they need.

HOW NOT TO SAY IT

1. Don't start preparing without a clear, compelling purpose in mind.
2. Don't give a presentation if you don't feel strongly about your subject.
3. Don't underestimate the value of knowing your audience.
4. Don't speak beyond the knowledge level of your core audience.
5. Don't assume all audiences are the same—or that they respond in the same fashion.
6. Don't take a "one-size-fits-all" approach; be flexible.

7. Don't speak on a subject unless you are qualified to do so.
8. Don't think you know it—till you know the outline—without the notes.
9. Don't take your speaking environment for granted.
10. Don't forget to review logistics with the technical crew.

3

Make Your Message Memorable

I saw a CEO end his presentation once with a slide that read, "The Sixteen Critical Areas for Success." During the question-and-answer session that followed, a senior partner stood up and asked, "What are the two or three things my people need to do back at the office?" The CEO struggled with his response and gave a long-winded answer. He couldn't boil down his message to a few key points, and he left his audience scratching their heads. In the political arena, look at what happened to John Kerry in the 2004 presidential election. George Bush was able to distill his message to one overarching theme—the war on terrorism and protecting America from future attacks. This approach resonated strongly with the American people. Kerry, on the other hand, tried a number of different messages and often got caught up in articulating the more complex, granular issues. Consequently, he couldn't clearly articulate why he was running and why people should vote for him.

What's the moral of these stories? Memorable messages need to be well-structured, clear, and simple.

AVOID INFORMATION OVERLOAD—SAY MORE WITH LESS

How do you ensure that your audience will remember your key points? Simple: don't say too much! If your main messages don't fit on the back of a business card, they probably won't be remembered. This means you're either covering too much material, or you're too far down in the weeds and haven't consolidated the content into broad themes or ideas. Remember, no matter how complex the topic, you need to be able to structure your thoughts in a clear and simple way to increase listener retention.

So while you may be inclined to tell the truth, the whole truth, and nothing but the truth, you don't have to give your audience everything and the kitchen sink, too! Resist the urge to throw in every last detail. In presentations, the more you say the less they'll remember.

Cut Out the Fat!

I once coached a senior accountant who, because of his professional training, wanted to include every fact and detail in his presentation. He came in with over sixty pages of text for a thirty-minute talk. We wound up spending the bulk of our time together making cuts rather than rehearsing. After several grueling hours, we deleted over half the material and got down to the core of his message.

Many presenters have a tough time trimming back to this bare-bones level, because it requires making difficult choices. But the end result is well worth the pain: your presentation (and message) becomes much more powerful. So how do you cut the fat without drilling into the bone?

To get to the essential elements of your message, here's some advice well worth remembering: Don't tell them what you want them to know. Don't tell them what they should know. *Tell them what they must not forget.*

GIVE THEM THE HEADLINES

It's always a good idea to tell your listeners at the start of your presentation what they need to remember—the key take-aways. This is an effective structuring tool that helps your audience store and remember important information. Headline the main points first before you elaborate on each. For example, "I want to cover three areas this morning: talent, development, and deployment." Once you've headlined the key points, elaborate on each one. *But:*

- Don't go beyond four or five main points. Even better, limit yourself to two or three if you can.
- Break down your presentation into small sections. Each section should consist of digestible chunks of information—this is much easier for listeners to remember. Don't overfeed them (just give them what they must not forget). You don't want your audience to leave your presentation feeling bloated!
- Check to see that your ideas flow in a logical sequence.
- Work in transitional phrases to link each section together. "Now let me start by telling you how we plan to deal with the current situation."
- Connect your points with a central theme such as, "Our Wheels Are in Motion," "The Opportunity of a

Lifetime," or "Determining Our Destiny Together." Keep in mind that themes are much easier for listeners to remember than pieces of isolated information.

- Recap and summarize along the way to ensure everyone is on the same page. For example, "We've talked about A, B, and C and realize why these are so important to our organization. Now let's take a look at D and see how this can differentiate us from our competitors."

- Keep your points punchy. Don't be long-winded. For example: "Management loves the proposal. Now let's talk about how we're going to finance this project."

- Determine how much time you should spend on each point or section. You want to have a well-balanced presentation.

OVERTIME DOESN'T PAY! PACE YOURSELF

Timing may seem mundane, but it's not. Most presenters don't time their remarks and they often go over—sometimes way over—their time allotment. This is the speaking equivalent of overstaying your welcome and it causes listeners to lose interest. Timing is essentially a discipline issue. As a presenter, you need to discipline yourself to take less of your audience's time. You're not only helping yourself, you're doing your audience a favor. Many presenters would do well to adhere to the time-honored show-business axiom "always leave your audience wanting more."

Unfortunately, many executives equate airtime with seniority. They often think, "the higher my rank, the more time I should get." But that's not how the audience thinks. If you're allotted sixty minutes for a presentation, talk for no more than thirty to forty minutes and reserve the remaining time for questions. If you come in a little under your allotted time, your audience will love you for it! For smaller client presentations you may want to allow even less time for prepared remarks and focus more on engaging the client in a meaningful dialogue. And don't rely on "guesstimating" the length of your presentation. What you think is thirty minutes may end up being more like forty-five. The only way to know for sure is to time yourself as you rehearse as well as during the actual presentation.

If you find you're more than halfway through your meeting and only a quarter of the way through your material, you have a problem. The likely culprit is (you guessed it) too much detail! Rise above it all with a ten-thousand-foot approach by focusing on the forest and not the trees. So if you're presenting from a book or slides, determine which pages or slides can be referenced quickly. Are there any that can be skipped entirely? Ideally, many of these decisions should be made *before* the meeting. But if you're running short of time during your presentation, you'll need to make these calls on the fly.

MAKE IT MEMORABLE WITH ANECDOTES, ANALOGIES, AND EXAMPLES

Like a good picture, a good anecdote or analogy is worth a thousand words. This is especially true when delivering complex or technical information. Yet all too often anecdotes and analogies are missing in action. Presentations without stories and personal examples are like food without seasoning; your material can become bland and dry.

Using interesting examples and analogies can really help clarify your point of view. I once heard Al Gore give a talk on global warming. If not treated the right way, a topic like this, while important, could generate a collective yawn. But Gore rose to the occasion. While his presentation was at times quite technical, he used vivid examples and interesting analogies that his audience could easily identify with, and thus made a scientific topic more accessible to everyone in the room. Without examples and analogies, it could have turned into a real snore.

Listeners always relate well to stories and personal experiences. They help make your presentation more interesting and memorable. But keep in mind that a good anecdote needs to fit the occasion. Don't throw one in at random. To be effective, an anecdote or analogy has to relate to your subject. For example, in a speech to teachers a CEO recently proposed strengthening the ties between business and education. Not everyone is comfortable with the concept of a partnership between business and academia. So to break the ice, the CEO made the following comment: "I know what you're thinking. Woody Allen may have summed it up best when he said, 'The lion and the lamb may lie down together, but the lion is going to get more sleep.' "

If appropriate, consider starting your presentation with an anecdote. This is a good way to capture your listeners' attention. It sure beats the standard, run-of-the-mill opening, "Good morning. Today I'd like to talk about . . ."

Keep an Anecdote Journal

Jot down interesting stories and experiences you hear from colleagues, as well as clients. Keep track of your own interesting experiences. When it comes time for your next presentation, decide which stories or experiences you want to share with your audience. Simply fold these into your presentation where appropriate. Make it a point to periodically update your presentation with new stories, analogies, and examples. It's a great way to keep your material fresh.

OWN THE OPENING

It's been said that what audiences remember most is the introduction and the conclusion. There is a certain amount of truth to this. This is not to say that what comes in between doesn't matter. It merely underscores the importance of the opening and closing of your presentation. Think of the first sixty seconds as the golden minute. It's when you can inspire confidence and assurance—or generate doubt and reservations. Blow it and you may lose your audience right from the outset.

Why do so many struggle with openings? I find a lot of professionals are highly competent when talking about the details of their business. Once they get into their technical area of expertise, they feel comfortable and confident. Yet they're often out of their element when they have to open a meeting or presentation because that's not where all the action is—it's not the meat of the presentation. As a result, they don't give it the time and attention it deserves.

A good introduction is like a good appetizer—it makes your audience enthusiastic about what follows. As the saying goes, you only get one chance to make a good first impression, so don't blow it. Here is a list of things to watch out for.

First-Impression Wreckers
- Jumping right into the presentation without a proper introduction.

- Missing the opening value statement, the "what's in it for me?" link that you want to make with your audience.
- Not structuring thoughts well; not framing issues well.
- Relying too heavily on notes, resulting in a lack of eye contact.
- Starting off with low energy and a lack of enthusiasm.
- Having little or no interaction with the audience.
- Using stiff body language.
- Showing discomfort with small talk.
- Speaking too fast (often caused by nervousness).
- Inserting too many "uhs" and "ums."

Many of these issues are covered in more detail later in the book. For now, let's focus on just a few.

Be Memorable from the Start

With a little creativity you can differentiate yourself from those who rely on the same old, same old ("Good morning, today I'd like to talk about . . ."). Instead, try one of the following options:

- Share an anecdote that is related to your topic. You don't have to tell a joke. Leave that to Jay Leno and David Letterman. Telling a joke is risky, and if it bombs you're left with egg on your face. A story or experience that is related to your topic is far safer and much more effective. If you want to interject some levity, self-deprecating humor is always a safe bet.
- Ask a question. It can be a rhetorical question or one that you want your audience to answer. "How many of you have ever heard of . . ."

- Share a personal observation. "I've been in this business for over twenty years but I've never seen anything like . . ."
- Provide a startling statistic. "Did you know that every seven seconds in this country . . ."
- Make a bold statement. "By the end of my presentation you will know the three key things we need to do to make us number one."

Tell "What's in It for Me?"

If you want to hold your audience's interest make it clear from the start why your presentation matters to them, and how they will benefit from what you have to say. Many people don't get to this until it's too late. Don't be subtle. Start off with a strong headline and tie it in to the needs and concerns of your audience. For example, "We've added six new modules to our programs this fall. So, what does this mean for you? It means you'll have more choices and for the first time, you'll be able to customize your courses to fit your own schedule. And that means no more late nights and long weekends!"

Frame the Issues and Agenda

Don't just dive straight into the details of your presentation. Take a step back and give your audience a quick preview of what's to come. Briefly outline the major points you intend to cover. For example: "There are three critical areas you need to be thinking about. These can make the difference between success and failure. They are A, B, and C. Today, we're going to walk you through each one of these, provide an in-depth analysis, and discuss why they're relevant to your operations." For small group meetings, prepare a few discussion questions in advance to involve your audience early on.

Make Small Talk

As if the formal part isn't enough, many presenters are also uncomfortable with making small talk and going off topic outside of the presentation. If you've ever presented, you know the feeling. There's often an awkward period before a meeting is set to begin, perhaps when people are still settling in, when you sense there's an opportunity to break the ice, but you don't quite know what to say. Small talk is a key business and social skill. It helps build rapport and establish common ground.

Small talk doesn't have to mean just talking about the weather. If you know the right techniques you can achieve a meaningful and rich dialogue with any audience. Here are a few guidelines to follow:

- Stay on top of the news. Scan the headlines. Keep abreast of current events and trends. Use a variety of sources including newspapers, magazines, radio, TV, as well as the Internet. (The Personal Journal section of the *Wall Street Journal* is a favorite of mine). This allows you to contribute by saying, "Yes, I saw a piece about that a few weeks ago. Is it true that . . ."
- Don't be single-minded; be well rounded. Know what's going on inside and outside your industry. Don't just focus on your specific area of expertise. Broaden your horizons and branch out a bit. The more you take in, the more interesting you are and the more you can add to a conversation.

- Listen attentively and link the conversation to a related topic. For example, "Speaking of great food, have you heard about . . ."
- Get to know the interests and hobbies of your clients. Focus on them, not yourself. If your client has a passion for baseball take a minute to check out the sports highlights.
- Start off with something you have in common or make a personal observation. "So, what did you think about the keynote speaker?" Or "I see you have one of those new-generation cell phones. Can you download songs on that?" Sometimes all you need is a good starter— the rest often takes care of itself.
- Prepare. Yes, you can actually prepare for small talk. Think of two or three potential things to talk about *beforehand*. You can even prepare a few follow-up questions.

Besides being a great ice-breaker, the ability to make small talk will serve you well during breaks and after the meeting or presentation is over. It's important to be an active participant during the meeting, but it's equally important to be part of the discussion when the conversation goes off topic. You don't want to be brilliant during the meeting, and end up with nothing to say when the focus shifts.

Send the Right Nonverbal Signals

Personal first impressions count as well. And the meter on you starts ticking from the moment you enter the room. Everything can make a difference—even the way you walk. So . . .

Mind your posture. Don't slouch. Stand up straight and keep your head up. Don't shuffle, walk with confidence. Be cognizant of your seated posture as well. Sit up straight, move in to the table, keep your arms in front of you, and lean in slightly toward your audience as you speak.

Maintain eye contact with your audience. When walking into a room, immediately make eye contact with your audience or client. Don't look down at the floor or off to the side. Maintain eye contact when shaking hands. If you look away too soon, you'll break this critical connection prematurely.

Give a firm handshake. Avoid the limp handshake at all costs—it has "weak and wimpy" stamped all over it. Put some passion in your grip! If you're presenting to a small group, make a point of shaking hands with everyone in the room. This is a great ice-breaker, as well as a great stress-reducer. It warms you up to your audience and warms them up to you before you officially begin your presentation. Think of it as the intro before the intro. When you look out at your audience and begin your opening remarks, you'll feel like you already know them—which is a very relaxing and comforting feeling.

BE A STRONG CLOSER

A weak close is like a disappointing dessert. It's unsatisfying and can even leave a bad taste in your mouth. Unfortunately, when it comes to presenting, the last thing you say is what you will most likely be remembered for. So don't cap off a really solid presentation by ending on a low note with something like, "Well, I think that should cover it. Any questions?" Talk about an anticlimax!

As with their openings, many presenters just don't spend a lot of time thinking about how they want to close. Think of it as your last chance to tie all the pieces together and reinforce your key message. It's where you can motivate, challenge, excite, or shake up your audience and inspire them to think, feel, or act in a new way.

How should you close? Consider linking your close to your opening remarks. Go back to the question you asked yourself when you first started preparing your presentation: "What do I want my audience to think or do when my presentation is completed?" Well, if you asked the question, now's the time to drive it home. Give your audience the answer. Restate your key points. Remind your listeners why your message matters to them.

Another option is to leave your audience with a thought-provoking line to remember—something that will resonate with them when they get back to the office.

Here's a good example: A hands-on CEO was making a presentation to his senior partners on the importance of leadership. He wanted his team to step up to the plate and start acting more like leaders instead of always waiting to be told what to do. He ended his talk by saying, "When I do it, it's micromanaging—when you do it, it's leadership." This resonated so well with the group that a number of partners chipped in and bought a plaque engraved with this quote, which they gave to the CEO to keep on his desk!

Don't Rush Your Ending

I've heard too many speakers speed up as they enter the homestretch and throw the ending away. It's as if they're saying, "Yeah, I finally made it, now I can go home!" As a rule, the pace of your closing remarks should actually be slightly slower than the body of your presentation. This is where you should underscore the importance of your words. Take your time. Pause when you need to for emphasis, and make every word count.

Own Your Closing

Try to memorize a portion of your closing remarks, just as you memorize your opening sixty seconds. You want to connect, eyeball to eyeball, with your audience as much as possible. If there is a question-and-answer period following your presentation, don't plan simply to end on the last question; it could be a downer. Always have a quick wrap-up ready to go that will leave your audience on a high note. For example, "There's no question we have some issues to resolve in the short term, but long term I see great potential ahead, and I fully expect our core businesses to generate double-digit returns over the course of the next three years."

In small group meetings, don't just wrap up by jumping to the "next steps" and "action plan." Before you address "where we go from here," make sure you all agree on exactly where "here" is. A good way to do this is to summarize together.

Don't Just Summarize, Synthesize!

Many speakers wrap up small group presentations by summarizing only what they've said and they neglect to incorporate the client's comments as they close. It's the difference between saying, "Here's what *I* covered" and saying "Here's what *we* covered." If you've been exchanging ideas throughout the presentation, doesn't it make sense to include the comments of others in your summary? Of course it does. For example, "We've weighed the pros and cons of a number of strategies. You've raised a number of important issues, including the logistical requirements of each concept. When we take all of this into account we believe the best solution is . . ."

Here's a novel idea: Involve the client in the recap. Let your audience tell you what they heard—and what they didn't hear. You can say something like, "Michele, what are your key take-aways from today's meeting?" Getting a recap through the ears and eyes of your client allows you to correct any misinformation or misunderstanding before it's too late.

HOW TO SAY IT

1. Determine two or three take-aways you want your audience to remember.
2. Cut the fat and get to the essential elements of your message. Tell your audience what they must not forget!
3. Give them the headlines up front.
4. Feed your audience digestible chunks of information.
5. Recap and summarize along the way.
6. Time your remarks.
7. Pace yourself. Decide where you need to go into detail, where you can briefly reference information, and which points you can skip.
8. Share interesting stories and personal examples and experiences.
9. Keep an anecdote journal.
10. Practice your opening and closing *out loud*.
11. Start off with an attention grabber.

12. Frame the issues in a way that shows why your presentation matters to the audience or client.
13. Send the right nonverbal signals when you enter the room.
14. Be a strong closer: Tie all the pieces together and drive home your key points. Leave your audience with a thought-provoking line they will remember.
15. Don't just summarize, synthesize! Fold in your client's comments as you wrap up.

HOW NOT TO SAY IT

1. Don't overload your audience with too much information.
2. Don't tell them everything you'd like them to know.
3. Don't go beyond your time limit.
4. Don't forget to time your run-through.
5. Don't leave out the stories and examples.
6. Don't gloss over your opening and closing remarks.
7. Don't jump right in without framing the issues in terms of how your presentation will benefit the audience.
8. Avoid standard openers such as, "Good morning, today I want to talk about . . ."
9. Don't discount the importance of the nonverbal signals you are sending.
10. Don't be a weak closer and end on a low note.
11. Don't forget to incorporate your client's comments in your wrap-up.

4

Presentation Pitfalls and How to Avoid Them

Great content, lousy execution. How many times have you given a presentation that didn't go over as well as it should have? You ask yourself what went wrong but you can't put your finger on it. It could be any number of things. Whatever the reason, I've seen many promising presentations fail because of a host of flawed strategies that in most cases can be easily fixed. Let's look at some of the probable causes and remedies.

PITFALL: RELYING TOO MUCH ON YOUR PRESENTATION DECK OR PITCH BOOK

People often tell me that some of the best presentations they've ever delivered were the ones where they never even opened a presentation book. (Presentation books generally contain visuals, speaking notes, or a script.) So don't feel compelled to dive into the book right from the start. In fact, it's often best to begin with some casual conversation. The advantage is that you get to know what's on the client's mind, and you get some insights into specific needs or concerns. Even if you may have spoken to the client a few days before the meeting and think you know what they want, it's still a good idea to let them talk first. What if an issue has suddenly arisen since your last conversation? This may change the focus of your entire presentation. If you uncover a pressing need, you may want to address this first, rather than starting on the first page of your presentation.

Prepare Some Premeeting Questions

Before you get to the meeting, put together a few questions that will help prompt a discussion with your client or audience. For example: "What is your current thinking on the new tax law and how do you think it will affect your company in the coming year?" or "How does your new management team feel about last year's strategy? Are they still on board?"

PITFALL: BECOMING A SLAVE TO THE PAGE

Some speakers bury themselves in their presentation books and become slaves to them. They go through their delivery page by page, covering every single detail ad nauseam. This can be dreadfully boring, as it gives the impression that you're wed to your script or notes at all costs. If you're not careful your audience will lose interest fast. What's the solution? Use your presentation book merely as a reference guide. Just because you've spent countless hours building your book, you shouldn't be a slave to it. Instead, pace your presentation. Determine ahead of time which pages need to be covered in detail, which pages can be quickly referenced, and which can be skipped altogether. You don't need to treat every page with the same level of detail. Consider putting together a one-page bullet-point outline for yourself covering the key points you want to make, then use it as a guide so you won't have to rely too heavily on your book.

Personalize Your Pages

Adding transitions at the top of your page will help you find the right words to introduce each page or visual. They don't have to be long. For instance, a good transitional heading about the timing of a merger could be: "Turning now to the timing of the deal." Another option is to write some personal notes in your book highlighting the key points you want to reference. For example, "Jen's quote from conference," "new marketing materials," "fiscal year highlights," etc. (If you're using a binder, you can write these down on the actual page, or jot down a few short bullets on the back of the previous page. So when you flip the page over, your notes appear on the opposite page.)

PITFALL: TOO MUCH CLUTTER

Don't overcrowd your pages with too much information because it puts your audience in an awkward bind. Think about it. You hand everyone a thick presentation binder. Do you want them reading through everything on the page or paying attention to you? Hint: *You*—not the book—should be driving the presentation.

So keep your presentation pages bare, and when designing your pages, leave plenty of white space. This gives you room to add personal notes and encourages your audience or client to follow you, not the book. If your company requires you to follow a certain template, you'll still have some freedom in terms of how you treat each particular page. Remember, you don't have to cover everything that's on the page. In fact, if you've got a busy page with lots of complex graphs and technical data, ask yourself, "What two or three points do I want my audience to remember?" A good way to address this would be to simply say, "There's lots of information on this page. For now, I want to focus on two key points."

Preview the Page or Visual

For complex pages or visuals, don't just start at the top and work your way down. Give your audience a preview of what it's all about. You can say something like, "This is a snapshot of what the new management reporting structure looks like. If you go to the box on the upper left side, you'll see . . ." As the presenter, you are in effect the audience's "chief information officer." It's your job to manage the flow of material both in terms of what to say and what to leave out.

Craft a Strong Headline to Spark Interest

A good headline grabs the attention of your audience and succinctly summarizes the content that follows. It should capture in a single, memorable line the essence of your message and make the audience want to hear more. Great headlines also tell the story of your presentation. If you had nothing on your pages but headlines, your story line should still be clear and the flow of logic should hold together.

Crafting headlines has other benefits, as well. It helps you organize your thoughts, as it forces you to distill your information and to focus on your core message. When developing your headlines, look for common themes that tie all the pieces together. Memorable headlines should use simple language and be easily understood. Keep your headlines short—less than ten words. Here are a few examples:

North American Revenue Jumps 15%
Service Sector Returns to Profitability
A Tipping Point for the Oil Industry
Public Relations Strategies Fail for Three Reasons

Dump the Details in the Appendix

When I tell people to keep their pages bare, I often get some resistance, mainly because they say their clients like lots of information. If that's the case, you should give your clients what they want. But instead of front-loading everything into your main presentation, consider creating an appendix at the back of your book to house all your data. An appendix solves two problems. First, it provides clients with a complete take-away document without cluttering up your presentation pages. Second, if the client wants more details about a specific issue, you can refer to the appendix at any time during the presentation.

PITFALL: TALKING TOO MUCH!

An investment banker recently complained to me, "I lose my train of thought when a client interrupts me in the middle of my presentation." I looked at her and said, "When the client does *what*?"

Here's a newsflash: Anytime a client wants to talk, stop
whatever you're doing and give him or her the floor. It's not
an interruption. And you shouldn't consider it an annoyance.
Think of it as a golden opportunity to learn what's on their
minds. You can gain valuable information about their specific needs—information that could help you better serve
them. So encourage them to interrupt, right from the very beginning of your presentation: "I'd like this to be an interactive discussion and want to encourage you to interject your
thoughts or questions at any time."

If your audience is bashful, don't be afraid to say it more
forcefully: "Please feel free to interrupt us at any time."
Your meeting will be much more productive and you'll enjoy a far richer dialogue if you make your audience part of
the discussion.

Of course, some clients won't need much prodding.
They'll let you know what's on their minds and freely interject throughout the presentation. But what do you do
when they're not very forthcoming? If you're doing all the
talking, it's time to pop some questions. Sometimes being a
good presenter means being a good interviewer. Below are
some ideas.

Learn to Ask Open-Ended Questions

- Don't just ask the obvious, "Are there any questions?" This is not a discussion starter. Use open-
  ended questions that get your clients talking. The
  more they tell you, the more you can help them. Try
  words and phrases such as "explain," "describe,"
  "walk me through," etc. Other questions you might
  consider:

"How would you evaluate the success of . . ."

"Suppose such-and-such happened, how would you deal with it?"

"How do you feel about . . ."

"How do you envision . . ."

- Plant open-ended questions in your presentation book. Think about what information would be valuable for you to have. Take some time to formulate these value-adding questions and decide where you want to insert them. Remember, the more probing your questions, the better the information you'll receive in return.
- If the initial response from your client is less than forthcoming, don't give up. Ask a follow-up question. Probe a bit until you get some good information.

Shut Up and Listen!

Talking too much is only part of the problem. Marching through your presentation like an advancing army can only compound the situation. There's only one way to fix this problem—pause to stop and listen to your client. Don't think of this as time away from your agenda. Sometimes you have to *break away* from your agenda and gather key information.

Listening is a skill that is often taken for granted. Perhaps that's why there are so many poor listeners around! Being a good listener requires the presenter to play a supporting role. This means you may have to temporarily put yourself to the side and allow the person who is speaking to take center stage, which is easier said than done.

Here are some of the most common listening problems I encounter, along with solutions to correct them.

Barriers to Effective Listening

- *Jumping in* before the other person has finished articulating a question, so you won't forget what you wanted to say.

    Remedy: Jot down a word trigger on a notepad to help you remember.

- *Becoming preoccupied with your reply* or rebuttal while the other person is still talking.

    Remedy: Clear your head and concentrate on what the other person is saying. If you're focusing too much on how you're going to respond, you're probably not paying enough attention to the other person. Give your brain more credit—it can formulate a good reply a lot faster than you think.

- *Feeling awkward when there's a break* in the conversation and compensating by constantly filling the airwaves.

    Remedy: Respect the silence. A moment of silence is usually a good thing. It allows you and the person you're interacting with time to reflect on what has been said.

- *Multitasking*—for example, checking your e-mail while talking on the phone, or even worse, checking your messages when someone is talking to you in person.

    Remedy: Give the person you're talking to your undivided attention. You simply won't listen as effectively if you're performing another task simultaneously. Besides, it's just plain rude.

- *Unnecessary distractions*, such as ringing cell phones or buzzing BlackBerries.

    Remedy: As they say in the airline industry, it's time to turn off all portable electronic devices, including cell phones, pagers, and BlackBerries. Listen in peace without interruption. The world is full of distractions and this is one you can easily control.

Learn to Listen Better

- Pick up on recurring ideas or themes. Listen for a connection between the points the other person is making. Draw on his or her earlier remarks, and work them into the conversation. "Peter, you've mentioned the importance of networking several times today. What can we do to help you enhance this process?" People are genuinely flattered to know you remember what they say.

- Empathize. Don't just extract cold data from your audience. Aside from the actual words, what is their tone or body language saying? When appropriate, acknowledge your audience's feelings. For example, "You sound frustrated with the current situation. I can understand why."

- Listen between the lines—to what is *not* being said. Sometimes what isn't said provides more valuable information than what is being said.

- Periodically restate information, by paraphrasing. It can be as simple as, "So what you're saying is . . ." When people hear their ideas played back it gives them an opportunity to clarify what they've said and ensures a mutual understanding of the issues.

- Communicate verbally that you're listening. Use such phrases as "I see," "Really?" and "Tell me more about . . ."

- Communicate nonverbally that you're listening. Maintain eye contact, nod your head, lean forward, match your facial expressions to the other person's words. Don't wear your poker face if they're telling you good news.

- Take brief notes. It's okay to jot down a trigger word or short phrase now and then. It will suppress the urge to interrupt because you won't have to worry about forgetting what the person has said or what you want to say. Referral notes can also provide a good summary of the discussion, and they're a good way of tracking earlier remarks by others—remarks that you can tie in later.

- Stop and think for a second before responding to a question. Resist the urge to jump right in. Pausing for a split second before you reply gives the impression of a more thoughtful answer.

- One final tip: Care enough to listen!

PITFALL: FAILING TO READ YOUR AUDIENCE

There seems to be a certain mystique about reading the spoken and unspoken signals your audience sends. I hear business professionals say things like, "Oh, Chris is really good at reading people." Or, "I'm just not a good people reader." It's as if this is some kind of innate skill that comes naturally to some but not others. Well, let's take the mystery out of it. Reading your audience is about being attentive—nothing more, nothing less.

Get Tuned In

If you have your head buried in your notes, you're not going to be able to read others. Conversely, if you're looking directly at your audience as you present, and if you're alert to what's going on around you, you'll have a much better chance of picking up important verbal and nonverbal signals. What are these signals and what do you do when you spot them? Here are a few to look for.

- **The Flipper** Someone is flipping a page or two ahead of you in the presentation book, indicating they want to move ahead. You may be spending too much time on the previous page.

  What to do: Consider going into less detail and highlight the main points instead. Use a big-picture approach.

  What to say: "Janet, would you like to move on to another issue?"

- **Dazed and Confused** Someone looks puzzled or confused, which means something isn't being understood. Perhaps your explanation is too technical or sophisticated. Or maybe you're not being clear and concise.

  What to do: Explain it again in simpler terms. This time use examples and analogies to move your story along.

  What to say: "Let's take a step back and review what we've just covered. Simply put, this is really about . . ."

- **The Fidgeter** Someone is fidgeting or looking at his or her watch.

  What to do: Propose taking a break or do a recap.

  What to say: "We've covered a lot of ground so far. Let's recap for a moment and then take a quick break."

- **Annoyed** Someone looks irritated. You've hit a hot-button issue.

  What to do: If appropriate, acknowledge the issue.

What to say: "I realize we're getting into a sensitive area here. How do you feel about . . ."

- **That Blank Look** Someone is disengaged and bored to death. Your presentation is dry, dull, too detail-oriented, or repetitious.

   What to do: Change your style and approach. Ask open-ended questions to engage your listeners. Modulate your voice to highlight the key points.

   What to say: "How do you envision rolling out this strategy?"

- **An Early Closer** If someone closes their book early in your presentation, it could be a sign your audience is bored, they've heard it all before, or they want to talk.

   What to do: Don't continue plowing through your presentation. Stop and shift your strategy. It's time to engage the client in off-book dialogue.

   What to say: "Gordon, we'll leave a copy of the book for you to review later. For now, what issues would you like to focus on?"

- **Note Takers** If people are nodding their heads and taking notes, rejoice! You're connecting with your audience, they're interested in what you're saying.

   What to do: Don't change a thing!

Good presenters are always aware of their audience. They strike a balance between focusing on the presentation and watching how it is being received. Make a conscious effort to be attentive to your audience. By the way, if you're presenting as part of a team, ask some of your colleagues who are not presenting at the moment to observe the verbal and nonverbal cues of listeners and report back to you during the break. Take advantage of every opportunity to gather real-time feedback on your audience.

PITFALL: NOT SPEAKING UP IN A FAST-PACED DISCUSSION

Picture this. You're involved in a fast-paced meeting where everybody is competing for airtime. You have something important to add, but there's no break in the conversation. You keep waiting for your chance to jump in. Next thing you know the conversation has shifted to a different topic and you've lost your opportunity to speak up. Sound familiar? What should you do? In situations like this, you have to be proactive; you have to interrupt. But how do you interrupt gracefully and politely?

Kill Them with Kindness: Break In with a Compliment

Let's face it, in today's highly competitive business environment most professionals aren't accustomed to being complimented in front of their peers. Pass the praise and you're pretty much guaranteed to shut the other person up even if it's for just a second, which should be just enough time for you to grab the spotlight. So a good way to leverage the power of positive feedback would be to forcefully say: "Great point, Sandy—there's another issue that we need to look at as well . . ."

By the way, interjecting with a compliment doesn't mean you have to agree with everything that has just been said. Once you get the floor, you can go in any direction you want. For example, "Great point, Sandy, although I'm not convinced the client will see it that way. What if we tried . . ."

Keep in mind that introverted personalities will need to really push themselves to interrupt. This is especially true for nonnative speakers from cultures where interrupting is considered impolite and disrespectful. The fact is, if you don't force yourself to speak up in meetings, others will think you have nothing to contribute, are not knowledgeable about the subject, or just not assertive enough. In American business you are expected to speak up and actively contribute to the meeting. Not doing so will hold you back!

Ask a Question

Posing a question is another way to make your voice heard, and it forces your listeners to address you directly. You then have an opportunity to follow up with a comment, such as, "What does this mean for the rest of the organization?" After they respond, you can follow up with, "I see. Then perhaps we need to look at how this will affect . . ."

PITFALL: HAVING LESS TIME THAN EXPECTED

If it hasn't happened to you yet, it will. You've planned for an hour-long presentation. But shortly before showtime you find out the event is running behind, or something unexpected has come up. Now you only have twenty minutes. What should you do? Talk three times as fast to cram everything in? (Don't laugh, some presenters have actually done this!) Your best option is to plan ahead, by determining *ahead of time* where you can make cuts. Wholesale edits are tough under the best of circumstances, but they're a lot harder on the fly.

Prepare a Plan B

Look at your presentation and ask yourself:

- Which parts can be skipped?
- Which can be referenced quickly?
- Where can you consolidate information?

Mark up your notes to indicate these changes. And remember our golden rule: Forget about what you would like them to know. Forget about what they ought to know. *Zero in on what they must not forget!* Aim for the highlights! Concentrate on the big picture. If your audience wants more detail, let them ask for it. And don't forget about questions and answers. Even when faced with severe time constraints, you should always allow time for questions. In fact, with only twenty minutes you might consider presenting just the executive summary and then use the remaining time to take questions. This is one of the best and most efficient ways to make your presentation relevant to the audience.

I recommend having a backup plan in place before you get to the event. This way you'll be ready for any last-minute changes, and your presentation will flow smoothly and seamlessly no matter what comes your way. Plus, you'll avoid the panic and mad scramble that unprepared speakers face. And best of all, your audience won't detect anything out of the ordinary.

PITFALL: BEING AS WOODEN AS AN OAK

Television newscasters are trained to look and sound natural when reading off a teleprompter. It's a skill that takes lots of training and sometimes years of practice to master. The pros make it look easy. However, most presenters who speak from a full text or straight narrative sound like they're reading. Their words come out flat and dry and carry little or no meaning. So what can you do to sound more natural and conversational when using a full script?

If you must speak from a full text, take the time to mark up your material.

- Using a pen or marker, highlight the most important words in each paragraph. Then modulate your voice on these key words for greater emphasis.
- Boldface key words you want to stress.
- Write in double slash marks (//) to indicate where to pause.
- Format your text so that each sentence starts on the left margin. This makes it easier for your eye to catch your next thought.
- Double-space your pages to allow plenty of white space.
- Practice out loud and tape-record yourself. Check to see that your delivery matches the markings you have made in your script.
- Record yourself again and strive for a conversational tone.

Use Bullet Points

A bullet-point outline generally encourages a more natural delivery and conversational tone. You can help your own cause by keeping your bullets brief—each bullet point should consist of no more than one key word or short phrase. Avoid lengthy sentences at all costs. When you're speaking, they'll tie you down to the text. Your eyes should be able to quickly glance down at your notes to catch a trigger word or phrase. Bullets are designed to jog your memory so you can finish the rest of the thought while maintaining eye contact with the audience. Use them correctly, and you should sound more like you're having a conversation and less like you're reading a speech. Of course, you need to know your material well enough to make this work.

Some feel an added sense of security speaking from a full text and are initially reluctant to move to bullets. They fear they might forget the thought or the words may not come out the way they want them to. A little practice time can easily rectify this. Besides, if you know your material well enough, you should be able to express your thoughts in a number of different ways. In most cases, as long as you get your main point across, it doesn't really make a difference which words you choose. Remember, it's not the individual words that count, it's how you communicate them that makes the difference!

Transition from Full Text to Bullets

Getting comfortable with a bullet-point outline is a simple process. If you follow the right steps you can ease your way into bullets and feel more confident about delivering your message in this format.

1. Write out every word of your presentation. Edit for content and ease of delivery. Say it out loud to make

sure everything feels and sounds right. Read it aloud a couple more times to learn and internalize the material.

2. Using a pen or marker, highlight the key words and phrases that capture the essence of each thought.

3. Create a first draft of a bullet-point outline using your highlighted words and phrases. Each bullet point should consist of a highlighted word or phrase. Practice out loud with the outline and see how well you can connect the dots. Practice until you feel secure.

4. When you become comfortable with your first draft of bullets, delete the points you no longer need and create your second and final draft. Practice until you feel comfortable and in control. Trust yourself!

Learn to Format Your Notes

- Double-space your text. Allow plenty of white space between each point. You shouldn't have more than five or six one-line bullets on a standard page. This makes it easier for your eye to grab each point.

- Use a font size that's easy to see (16 to 18 points usually works well).

- Mark up your notes for emphasis (underline, bold, double slashes, etc.).

- If you're using index cards, reduce the number of points on each card so you have sufficient white space and your cards are not cluttered.

- Mark where visual aids are going to be used.

- Always, always number your pages—they have a way of getting out of order.

PITFALL: POWERPOINTING YOUR PRESENTATION TO DEATH

Do you suffer from PowerPoint-itis? It seems you can't go to a presentation these days without being overwhelmed by endless displays of bullets, graphs, and related visual pyrotechnics. The good news about PowerPoint is we've come a long way from the days of cheesy overheads and fragile glass-mounted slides. But the bad news is that PowerPoint has become a debilitating crutch for many a presenter. Visuals should never be the centerpiece of your presentation. At best, they should play a supporting role. How do you know if your visuals are overshadowing you, and your presentation? Here's a simple test. Try practicing your presentation without any visuals. If it doesn't hold together well, you're letting PowerPoint run the show. If you think about it, the most powerful speeches in history never needed visuals. Why? The strongest visual has always been and will always be you, the speaker. Nonetheless, if you must use visuals, avoid these common mistakes.

The Seven Most Common PowerPoint Bloopers and How to Avoid Them

- *Too Many Visuals* If you're giving a thirty-minute presentation, you shouldn't have forty-five visuals! Use visuals only if there's a compelling reason to do so—perhaps to illustrate a new structure that your audience really needs to see, or maybe a complex idea that needs to be shown in a simple, clear fashion. Many presenters use visuals as their personal talking points, which only succeeds in creating a lot of unnecessary visuals. Remember, the whole world doesn't need to see your notes. In fact, the only thing your audience should be paying full attention to is you.

Remedy: When in doubt, use fewer visuals. Cut, cut, cut! Create a one- or two-page talking-point outline that you can keep nearby as a reference guide. The bulk of your data should be in a leave-behind document, not in your visuals.

- *Too Much Information on Each Visual* What's the point of having a visual if no one in the room can read it? I've seen visuals so crammed with information that you would need a pair of binoculars to make them out. Pack your visuals to the brim and your audience will struggle to decipher what's on the slide while you're trying to make your point. You may have a memorable presentation on your hands but it won't be for the right reasons.

  Remedy: Limit the amount of information on your visuals. Don't go beyond three to five points per page. Use one to two lines per point. Try not to have more than twenty words on a visual. Aim for phrases rather than full sentences. Use large print and easy-to-read fonts. Apple CEO Steve Jobs writes and designs many of his own slides and is a master at visual presentations. His visuals are simple, clear, and uncluttered. He often has just one or two words on a slide, which gives his message much greater impact. When he uses multiple lines of text, only one point is highlighted at a time; the rest fade out so listeners stay focused on his current thought. If you want to see a persuasive presenter in action, I suggest you check out one of his webcasts.

- *Reading Visuals Verbatim* Few things are more annoying (and boring) than listening to someone recite the same words that are on each visual. What's the point? Your audience can read just as well as you can.

  Remedy: Paraphrase what's on each visual. Elaborate using examples, anecdotes, and analogies.

- *Talking to the Visuals and Not the Audience* Don't talk directly to your visuals. Because when you do, you've got your back turned to your audience and that's never a good idea. It breaks the connection between speaker and listener. And it also makes your words harder to hear since you're projecting your voice backward rather than out in front to your listeners.

  Remedy: When referencing something in your visual, turn your body at an angle so your back is not to your audience. Stop speaking as your head turns to the visual. Reference the point on the visual, then turn back to the audience and resume speaking so you can maintain eye contact with your listeners. The same holds true when using a laptop. Don't talk as you look down to advance the presentation. Pause for a second, hit the proper key, reestablish eye contact, and resume speaking. Also, don't point too much. In most cases, your audience knows where to look based on what you are saying. If your visuals are clear and simple, you shouldn't have to continuously point to the screen with your finger.

- *Overly Complicated Charts and Graphs* Charts, graphs, and tables are supposed to simplify information, not make it more complicated. If your graphic requires a lengthy explanation you probably need to find a way to simplify it.

Remedy: Keep all charts, graphs, and diagrams clear and simple. And be sure to make them large enough so your audience can easily read the data points.

- *Too Much Animation* We really don't need to hear all those silly sound effects, or see the moving arrows, flying text, etc. These are unnecessary distractions. They detract from your basic message.

  Remedy: Ease up on all the bells and whistles. The animation is in the wrong place—it should come from you, the presenter, not the PowerPoint presentation.

- *Not Rehearsing with Your Visuals* Whenever technology is involved, expect the unexpected.

  Remedy: Check to see that all your visuals are in order. Make sure you or someone else knows how to operate the equipment. Go through your entire presentation, visual by visual, to iron out any kinks in the system. Make sure everything is working properly on the day of the presentation. Always have the telephone extension of a technician handy, as well as a hard copy of your presentation for a backup.

HOW TO SAY IT

1. Begin with some off-book dialogue.
2. Prepare some premeeting questions.
3. Use your book as a reference guide.
4. Personalize your pages.
5. Ask open-ended questions to get the client talking.
6. Know when to shut up and listen.
7. Be on the lookout for important verbal and nonverbal cues from your audience.

8. Politely interrupt to get your point across in a fast-paced discussion.
9. Always have a Plan B.
10. Practice speaking naturally from notes.
11. Make sure your visuals play a supporting role.

HOW NOT TO SAY IT

1. Don't bury yourself in your presentation book.
2. Don't be a slave to the page.
3. Don't clutter up your pages with too much information.
4. Don't view client comments as interruptions.
5. Don't do all the talking.
6. Don't ask yes/no questions.
7. Don't take your listening skills for granted.
8. Don't miss important verbal and nonverbal signals from your audience.
9. Don't sit through a presentation without saying anything.
10. Don't go to a meeting or presentation without a Plan B.
11. Don't sound like you're reading your presentation.
12. Don't rely too heavily on your visuals.

5

Setting the Stage

You've prepared well. You feel good about your content. You've learned how to steer clear of common pitfalls. You're finally ready to present, right? Well, almost. Before launching into your presentation, there are still a few things you need to think about, issues that will determine your style and approach and how well you relate to your audience. For example, will you be speaking from a podium? How skillful are you at using a microphone? How will you handle questions from the audience? These are not just peripheral issues, they can actually have a dramatic impact on how you and your presentation are received.

USING A PODIUM EFFECTIVELY

Some speakers say the podium cramps their style. Others like it because it gives them something to hide behind. Either way, it's possible to find a happy medium. If you use a podium, you should make the most of it. In the political arena, the podium is often a candidate's best friend. For example, former president Bill Clinton is one of the best podium speakers around. Even from behind a podium, he looks perfectly natural. At the Democratic National Convention in 2004, there was nothing stilted or stiff about his speech. His upper body was loose and fluid. He periodically shifted his weight and used broad gestures as he spoke. His face and voice were always expressive. In fact, for much of his talk, it appeared as though Clinton wasn't even using a podium. With a bit of practice you, too, can become comfortable and speak more naturally with a podium. After all, you never know when you may have to use one. How do you use a podium properly? Here are some pointers.

- Don't cling to the top of the podium for dear life! Some speakers grab on to the sides of the podium and never let go. This can make you look tight, tense, and nervous. Free yourself. You don't need to physically engage with the podium. Think of it simply as a resting place for your notes. You can stand back a few inches and let your arms and body move freely. There's no need to feel boxed in.
- If you prefer making contact with the podium, simply rest your fingertips on the bottom edge of the podium surface by the lower lip. Make this home base for your hands when you're not gesturing. Since podium surfaces are slanted slightly downward, no one in the audience will even see your fingertips resting there. This free and loose position allows for maximum ease of movement.

- Consider positioning yourself to the side of the podium. There's no rule that says you have to stay behind the podium the whole time. If you know your talk well enough, you can glance down at your notes, step away, and deliver your remarks off to the side of the podium. As you complete your thought, take a step back (still facing your audience) and glance down again to grab your next point.

- Don't turn your page over when you get to the bottom; it's too obvious to your audience. Instead, gently slide each page across to the other side. This looks a lot smoother and no one will know how many pages you are using.

- If you're using a script, make sure the surface area of the podium is wide enough to accommodate two standard sheets of paper resting side by side. Podium sizes and styles vary widely, so it pays to check in advance. Find out if the podium is already set up with a laptop computer. If this is the case, you'll have a lot less room for your notes, so consider using index cards instead. Also check to see if there is a lip at the bottom of the surface so your notes won't slide off while you're speaking. You can easily have one constructed or you can even make your own lip by folding over some masking tape several times to form a ridge.

- When talking to very large audiences such as at a major conference, some people prefer speaking from a teleprompter instead of using hard copy. In this arrangement, transparent glass panels, attached to both sides of the podium, display your text. This technology allows you to look out at your audience and catch your words on the side panels at the same time.

When done right, it can give the impression that you are not looking down at your notes as you would with a hard-copy script. However, mastering the teleprompter is a skill that requires practice. For more on how to effectively use this technology, see page 120.

- Make sure the podium has sufficient light—and that it doesn't shine in your eyes or cast a shadow over your notes.

- Check to see that the podium microphone is working and is adjusted at a height and angle that works best for you. (If you're following someone who's either taller or shorter, you may need to adjust the height of the mike.) Talk to the sound engineer about how best to handle this. If you're going to periodically walk away from the podium, make sure you have a clip-on microphone that works properly. Ask the sound people if there's a chance you'll hear feedback if both the podium mike and clip-on mike are turned on simultaneously.

Breaking Free of the Podium

Just because there's a podium in the room, it doesn't mean you have to use it. In fact, many speakers see the podium as a barrier between them and their audience, and they prefer to walk around instead. They feel freer and more natural presenting away from the podium. I often refer to this as the Phil Donahue or Oprah Winfrey style of presenting. And in many cases it's a perfectly good option.

In fact, at the 1996 Republican National Convention Elizabeth Dole (the wife of former senator Bob Dole) used this approach very effectively. Unlike all the other speakers, who spoke from behind the podium, Dole broke with tradition and walked her way down from the main stage right into the audience. A wireless microphone allowed her to move freely through the crowd. Even more importantly, it instantly set her apart from all the other speakers. Because Dole was closer to her audience she was able to personally connect in a way that speakers up on the big stage couldn't. This technique also made her appear more down to earth— she was now "one of them." Instead of looking stately and presidential, she came across as a personable, warm, and welcoming host. It worked like a charm.

Will it work for you? Remember that you can walk around without jumping into the crowd. Many times it's best to stay in front of your audience while you move about. This works whether you're on a stage or a raised platform or just standing on the floor. There are a few things you should keep in mind when speaking without a podium. If you're going to walk around, be careful not to pace back and forth. Instead, move with a purpose. If you do walk the room, don't delve too far into the crowd—you don't want to turn your back on the people in the front section for too long. It's always better to spend the majority of your time in front of your audience. This gives you—and them—the best vantage point. If you need to advance a visual, and you're too far away from your laptop, have a backup plan in case your remote conks out (I've seen this happen a number of times). Or better yet, consider designating someone to change your visuals. If you're using a remote pointer to reference a piece of information, don't zigzag the light beam on the visual, just make one circular motion to highlight your data point. Finally, if you're going to move away from the podium, you may want to use some note cards. You don't want to be looking back at your slides too frequently as you present. Jot down a few bullet points on each card (four-by-six-inch index cards usually work well). You should know your material well enough so that a quick glance at your bullets will jog your memory for the complete thought. Be sure to rehearse with your note cards and remember to number each card. If you're speaking at a large conference, you may also have the option of using floor monitors. In such a case, television monitors, typically placed on both sides of the stage, display your text. Depending on the available software, you can either have scrolling text or PowerPoint slides. As stated earlier, to pull this off smoothly, you'll need to allow sufficient practice time to master the technique.

Here's another option to consider: combine the podium and nonpodium approaches. For example, you might begin your introductory remarks from the podium as a way of establishing yourself, and then walk around for the core of your presentation. You can then make your way back to the podium for your closing remarks as a way to reestablish yourself and close out the session. In some cases, the formality of the occasion dictates which strategy to use. For formal affairs, speaking from a podium may be more appropriate. But in most cases, it's really up to you to decide. Many of my clients prefer speaking away from the podium because it frees them up and they feel more natural. So, which method should you use? I've laid out the pros and cons of each approach. The best strategy is to experiment with different options and see what works best for you.

USING A MICROPHONE PROPERLY (PREVENTING MICROPHONE MISHAPS)

We've all witnessed the unlucky speaker who starts speaking into a microphone only to realize that it's not turned on. Here are a few guidelines that can help you avoid and/or prevent some of the most common microphone mishaps:

- Before you begin speaking into a microphone, make sure it's plugged in! Check for an on/off switch. The best way to test a microphone is to speak into it. Either count off a few numbers or just say "testing, testing." Blowing into or tapping against a microphone can actually damage the mike and hurt the ears of your audience.
- If possible, do an advance sound check. Find a sound engineer or someone who has the expertise to help you. If you can't find anyone, you can adjust your volume by your proximity to the microphone. Start off about six inches away from the mike and see how you do. If the sound is too loud, back away a little. On the other hand, if you're having a hard time being heard, you can move in a little closer. Doing a sound check is always a smart idea because it gives you a sense of just how powerful the amplification will be. If you're not accustomed to using a mike, a little practice will help you get comfortable with the sound and feel of your amplified voice.
- Keep in mind that every microphone is different; some are more sensitive to sound than others. The key is learning to adjust your distance to the microphone to get the best sound. If you speak too closely into a mike your words may become fuzzy and garbled. This creates distortion. It can also cause feedback, that dreaded high-pitched, ear-piercing noise that occurs when

there's an overload of sound. In most cases, the sound is too loud. If you run into feedback, back away a little.

- Be aware that when a sudden rush of air hits a microphone it can create a jarring sound for listeners. We've all heard them—even the smallest distractions can feel like thunder when they're amplified. So if you have to cough, sneeze, or clear your throat, make sure you turn your head away from the microphone. Also, watch out for "popping p's." If you hear a tiny explosion every time you say the letter "p," adjust your position slightly. Don't talk directly into the microphone. Talk across it instead, and try not to hold it with your hand. If you're wearing a microphone that's clipped on to your clothing, be aware that any gesture or movement that touches the mike or clothing near the mike will often cause a distracting noise. So avoid hitting your chest or adjusting a tie, jacket, or necklace while the mike is on.

- Always assume your microphone is on. Don't say anything next to a microphone that you wouldn't want everybody in the room to hear. Many an unsuspecting speaker has paid the price for making insulting or off-color comments while their mikes were on.

Here is one additional note of caution. Be especially careful with wireless clip-on microphones. If you're using a wireless lavaliere mike, always remember to turn it off when you're not presenting. A colleague was teaching a leadership course to an all-male group of financial executives who were overworked and cranky. It was the very first time she had used a wireless mike. During a break she went to the ladies' room still wearing her mike and didn't realize it was still recording. You guessed it—all the background noise from the bathroom got piped into the conference room. Someone had to call the HR director to go into the ladies' room and get her out. Needless to say, she was mortified. When she returned to the room, no one said anything at first. The silence was unbearable. Then, one guy looked at another guy sideways and started laughing. Next thing you know there was loud, explosive laughter. The whole room went nuts. After that, it turned out to be a great course. Fortunately for the trainer, this had a happy ending, but you may not be so lucky. Lesson learned? Take your mike off when you're not speaking.

GETTING THE MOST OUT OF Q&A SESSIONS

In chapter 4 we looked at effective questioning techniques in small group meetings. Now let's consider the same issue for larger audiences.

If You Want Questions, Be Proactive

What happens when you ask for questions and no hands go up? This can be an awkward moment. Many presenters typically wait a second or two, look around the room, and then finish up by saying something like, "Well, if there are no questions, then I guess that wraps it up." This is a weak way to end a presentation, and it's a missed opportunity to hear from your audience. The way you ask for questions can make a big difference. Let's face it, "Are there any questions?" doesn't sound very inviting. Instead, move in toward your audience, maintain eye contact, raise your hand up high, and say with an enthusiastic tone, "Who has the first question?" Or "What questions do you have for me?" If no hands go up at this point, don't panic. Have a few questions of your own ready in your back pocket. "One question I often get asked is . . ." You can either answer the question yourself or ask if anyone in the audience has any thoughts on it. This helps get the momentum going. Chances are there will be something in your question that will trigger a related or follow-up question from the audience.

Always Repeat the Question

Have you ever been in the audience when someone asks a question and the speaker starts answering even though half the people didn't hear the question? Pretty frustrating, isn't it? Don't make this mistake. When taking questions in large group settings, always repeat the question, simply by stating, "The question is, What is our game plan for the next twelve to eighteen months?" This ensures that everyone hears the question and it also buys you a few extra seconds to formulate your response.

Handling Complex Questions

If you get a complicated question that you don't understand or a portion of your audience might not understand, politely ask the person to rephrase the question.

Say, "I'm not exactly clear about what you are asking. Would you kindly rephrase the question?" If you feel the person is still not clear, restate the question in simpler terms yourself; for example, "I believe what you're asking is, 'What are the implications of the new tax codes?' Is this correct?"

Responding to a Negative Question

If you get hit with a negative question, don't get defensive. Stay calm, collected, and positive. You may want to rephrase or redirect the question.

For instance, if you are asked, "Why isn't management doing more to train and develop our people?" you could respond, "Training and developing our people has always been a top priority for us. We know how important it is for all of you as well. We've recently initiated a number of new programs that we plan to roll out this fall. Because we're a big organization the process is not always as fast as we would like, but rest assured we're very committed to developing our people to their fullest potential."

When You Don't Know the Answer to a Question

Don't feel obliged to answer a question that falls outside your area of expertise. Remember, you're there to talk about what you know—not about what you don't know. If you don't know the answer, it's okay to admit it. By the same token, don't try to be a "know it all" and fabricate one on the spot. This can erode your credibility. Simply say, "I don't know the answer to that off the top of my head. Let me check on it and I'll get back to you as soon as I can." If you feel confident someone else in the room knows the answer, you can defer to an expert on your team or an audience member. You can also transition to something you do know. For example, "I'm not familiar with the details on that specific project, but I can tell you about a similar one where we've had great success."

Link the Question to a Point
You Want to Make

If someone asks a question that doesn't really address the issue at hand, briefly respond to the immediate question then
redirect it to a point you want to make by using phrases
such as:

"The real issue is . . ."
"The main point is . . ."
"The fact is . . ."
"More importantly . . ."

This technique is called "bridging." It gets you back to
your main point quickly and seamlessly. One of former
president Clinton's favorite bridging techniques is to say,
"The critical issue you need to understand is . . ."

Don't Cut Off the Questioner

Even if you know the answer halfway through the question, don't cut the questioner off in midsentence. Let the
question come out on the table before you respond. As you
answer, make eye contact with others in the room; don't
just look at the questioner the whole time.

Pause before Responding

Resist the temptation to jump right in after you hear the
question. A knee-jerk response can get you off to a poor
start. It can also make your answer appear rehearsed.
Don't feel rushed. Pause for a second before you respond.

This allows time to gather your thoughts, and creates the impression of a more thoughtful answer.

Don't Overanswer

After you've fully answered a question or made your point, stop talking. I once observed a CEO handling questions after a major client presentation. I decided to time his answers. It turned out that a number of his responses lasted more than four minutes! By the time he completed an answer, it was hard to remember what the question was. The problem with being thorough is that long-winded answers aren't memorable. Whenever possible, be brief and get to the point quickly.

Handling Questions from a Large Audience

If you're speaking to a large audience, consider collecting written questions in advance of your presentation. These can be recorded on index cards. You can then screen the questions and formulate your answers ahead of time. Make an effort to take a few live questions from the audience as well so the Q&A period won't appear canned.

Handling Two- or Three-Part Questions

A CEO from a leading professional services firm was once asked a two-part question during a live TV interview which went something like, "How are you going to attract top talent to your firm given all the ethical problems associated with your profession? And can you tell us what percentage of your business comes from consulting?" He responded by saying, "Well, it's tough to say for sure, but . . ." At this point the interviewer chimed in and said,

"You mean to say you don't know for sure how much of your business comes from consulting?" Clearly, the CEO was responding to the first question, but he neglected to reference this before he responded. If you're asked a two- or three-part question, always reference the part of the question you're going to answer first. Simply say, "Let me respond to the first part of your question . . ." If by the time you finish answering the first part of the question you've forgotten the second part, you can always ask the questioner to repeat it.

Structure Your Responses

Always try to give some structure to your answers, especially if you have to make more than one point. For example, "There are three points that need to be addressed here. One is investors. Two is the supply situation. Three is demand." Sometimes it's difficult to structure your thoughts up front, especially when you're thinking on your feet. If you find you're not heading down a clear path, you can often provide structure at the end of your response as you summarize. For example, "So, it really boils down to A, B, and C."

Prepare a List of Anticipatory Questions

Too many times I hear after the fact, "Gee, I wasn't expecting that question." This is just a weak excuse for poor preparation. Part of your job as a presenter is to predict—as well as possible—what questions may come your way. No one can read minds, but you can take much of the guesswork out of the process by putting yourself in the shoes of your audience. Keeping in mind the background, knowledge levels, and biases of your listeners, think of the questions they would most likely ask. Be sure to include the tough questions. Then prepare a response for each one. Simply jot down a few bullets to briefly outline your answers. Make this part of your rehearsal process. If you run out of gas, turn to someone who knows the subject and ask him or her to speculate about possible questions. Murphy's Law sometimes goes hand in hand with question-and-answer sessions. It's usually the question you think you're most likely to hear that doesn't get asked.

Don't Close on the Last Question

If you intend to have a question-and-answer session following your presentation, don't end on the final question. The last question may be a bit of a downer or it may focus on an issue that doesn't tie in well with the key theme of your talk. It's always stronger to close with a brief summary or call to action. One minute or less is okay. It puts you in the driver's seat and allows you to end on a high note.

GETTING FEEDBACK YOU CAN USE

One of the best ways to measure your progress as a presenter is by getting feedback from your colleagues. Unfortunately, if you ask most people for feedback on your performance, the typical response is usually, "I thought you did well." This really doesn't provide much meaningful information. To get valuable feedback—feedback you can really use—you need to ask for it *before* the meeting or presentation. Ask someone you trust to focus on one or two *specific* things, such as, "I'm working on speaking slower and cutting down on my 'ums' and 'uhs.' At the end of the meeting can you let me know how I did?"

Now the person knows precisely what to look or listen

for *ahead of time* and can better evaluate your performance. You're guaranteed constructive feedback and you'll be able to more accurately measure your progress going forward.

HOW TO SAY IT

1. Get comfortable speaking from a podium in case you need to use one.
2. Feel free to walk around and present away from the podium.
3. Consider combining the podium and nonpodium approaches.
4. Do a sound check to test the microphone.
5. Always assume your microphone is on.
6. Always turn off your wireless clip-on microphone when you're not presenting.
7. Gently slide your pages on the podium to the side when you're finished using them.
8. Ask for specific feedback *before* the presentation.
9. In larger group settings, always repeat questions from the audience.
10. Be ready to start the Q&A momentum by offering a question you're often asked.
11. Respond to a question only when it's been asked in its entirety.
12. If you get hit with a negative question, stay calm, collected, and positive. Consider rephrasing or redirecting the question.
13. If you can't answer a question, it's okay to admit it. Offer to find the answer and get back to the person as soon as you can.

14. When responding to questions be brief—get to the point and move on.
15. Rather than closing your presentation on the last question, offer a brief summary or call to action.
16. Prepare a list of anticipatory questions and practice your responses.

HOW NOT TO SAY IT

1. Don't feel obligated to use a podium just because there's one in the room. If you walk around, don't delve too deeply into your audience—you may lose people up front.
2. Don't let a podium cramp your style.
3. Don't cling to the podium for dear life.
4. Don't skip the sound check before you speak.
5. Don't test a microphone by blowing into or tapping against it.
6. Never say anything near a microphone that you wouldn't want everybody in the room to hear.
7. Don't leave your wireless microphone turned on when you're not presenting.
8. Don't turn your page over when you get to the bottom of it.
9. Don't open your question-and-answer session with a nonstarter that's likely to bomb, such as "Are there any questions?"
10. Don't start answering a question before it's fully asked.
11. Don't get defensive if you're hit with a negative question.
12. Don't feel obligated to answer a question that falls outside your area of expertise.

13. Don't overanswer.
14. Don't close your presentation on the last question. It can be anticlimactic.
15. Don't get caught by a question you weren't expecting. Be prepared.

6

Thinking Quickly: On a Panel or On the Spot

Life would be simple if there was only one type of presentation to prepare for. Yet the reality is most professionals will face a host of different speaking situations in their careers and each requires a unique set of skills to master. As you'll see in this chapter and the one that follows, different types of presentations often require different strategies and approaches. Here we'll focus on panel discussions as well as how to think on your feet.

PRESENTING ON A PANEL

As a panelist you need to strike the right balance between saying too much and not enough. If you think about it, the job of a panelist really begins when the prepared remarks end. This is when you need to actively listen and look for places to interject your thoughts. You also need to be respectful and give your fellow panelists a chance to talk.

Don't Be a Silent Spectator

I once coached a top executive who was invited to be part of a high-profile panel in China. I watched a videotape of one of his previous panel discussions and immediately saw the problem. After he completed his opening remarks, he basically sat there in silence for the remainder of the session (with the exception of a few very brief closing comments). His head went back and forth as he listened to other presenters but he said nothing. He could have been watching a tennis match.

Presenting on a panel is not a spectator sport. You can't sit on the sidelines—you have to be part of the action. So as the discussion unfolds think about how you can add on to another panelist's answer. You might say something like, "Just to add one point to Bob's comment, another issue to consider is . . ." Remember, you can't always wait for the moderator to invite you into the discussion.

Don't Be a Talk Hog

On the flip side, there are panelists who don't seem to know when to stop talking. They feel compelled to respond to every single question and often wind up dominating the discussion. They waste everybody's time saying things that have already been said and their responses go on forever. They take center stage when they should be sharing the stage. Needless to say, this is extremely annoying and frustrating to the audience, as well as other panelists. A good moderator should be able to control the motormouths. But you can do your part by not hogging the spotlight.

Becoming an Effective Panelist: Guidelines to Follow

So what does it take to be an effective panelist? Like any form of presentation, it takes solid preparation and the correct techniques. Here are some guidelines that will help you become a more effective presenter:

- Will you be giving introductory remarks? If so, how long or short should they be? The organizer or moderator will usually tell you long before the panel discussion actually occurs. But if for some reason you don't know, a good rule of thumb is to keep your introductory remarks to two minutes or less. When you're speaking, take special pains to tone down the sales pitch. Remember, you're not there to brag; you're there to inform and enlighten. Say something that really matters to your audience. When in doubt, use the "so what?" approach: put yourself in the audience's shoes and ask yourself why they should care about what you have to say. Do a dry run of your prepared remarks and *time yourself*. Nobody enjoys listening to a long-winded panelist.

- Make sure the moderator has a copy of your bio, and consider highlighting the key points you would like him or her to mention. For example, if you've written a new book it's not unreasonable to ask the moderator to reference the title and publisher when you're introduced.

- Where are you in the order of presenters? Being last isn't necessarily a bad thing. While it's true that a lot of ground may already have been covered by other panelists, there are a number of advantages to appearing later. For example, you'll have more time to formulate a response. You can incorporate the remarks of other presenters into your response. You may have the last word. (Don't underestimate how important that is, given what we know about what audiences remember most.) Also, if the panel has just reviewed a lot of data, you may have an opportunity to provide an interesting example, anecdote, or observation to illustrate the point and tie all the pieces together.

- Keep a notepad nearby with a few bullets outlining the key points you want to make. Use it as a quick reference guide during the discussion. Remember, your job is not simply to answer questions, but to convey your two or three take-aways. You need to be able to weave your main points into your responses.

- When responding to questions, keep your answers concise. Make sure you can see the moderator out of the corner of your eye, and be cognizant of any signals you may be receiving to wrap things up. Don't put the moderator in a position of having to jump up and down to get your attention.

- Be an active listener. Pay attention to the points other panelists are making. On your notepad, jot down trigger words and phrases so that you can refer back to their comments later on. You can definitely score some big points if you can reference their remarks *and* use their names. For example, "As Marsha said earlier, it's really not a zero-sum game anymore. This is especially true now that . . ."

- Always make eye contact with your audience when you respond. Regardless of who asks a question, don't focus on the moderator or a fellow panel member when you respond. If a participant criticizes something you've said, briefly tilt your head in their direction to acknowledge where the remark came from. But resist the temptation to turn and direct the bulk of your response to that person. Instead, look at your audience and direct your comments to them.

- Don't disengage when you're not speaking. I've seen too many panelists just tune out when other panelists are talking. Their body language says "gone fishing." Don't slouch or get too laid back in your chair. (This looks like you don't care about what others have to say, and it sends a negative message to your audience. It's also disrespectful.) Whether you're speaking or not, you're always in full view of the audience and other panel members. Even when you're not talking, your body language is always communicating. So don't play with your pen or pencil, and by all means don't multitask. (Don't even think of looking at your BlackBerry.) Also, never talk to another panelist while someone else is speaking. Force yourself to stay involved.

WHEN YOU ARE THE MODERATOR

As a moderator, you're in charge of the panel discussion. Your job is to engage the panelists in interesting dialogue and to generate a compelling discussion. Like a good emcee, you need to keep things moving and make the session interesting for the audience.

Be clear about your role. You should be acting more as a facilitator than a panelist. Resist the temptation to answer questions and offer opinions. Your job is to guide and steer the discussion, not to get overly involved in it. You also act as a mediator for the panelists.

Once the theme and topics for the panel discussion have been determined, you need to set guidelines. Set up a conference call in advance with all the participants so that everyone can agree on basic rules of the road such as:

- What particular issues should be addressed (Note: Sometimes it's best not to give your exact questions to panelists in advance since this can make their answers appear rehearsed and detract from the spontaneity of the moment)
- The individual roles participants will play based on their expertise
- Logistical matters such as timing

Set the Ground Rules

Set the ground rules early. Tell participants how you would like to run the session. Each panelist should have a clear understanding of how much time they have for their opening remarks, how much time will be reserved for discussion, and how long the question-and-answer session will take. Explain how you would like them to interact with each other. You may want to discourage presenters from speaking to each other across the table, and remind them to address all their remarks directly to the audience.

Consider the Seating Arrangement

Don't underestimate how important seating arrangements can be in a panel setting. Seating panelists in a straight row is not always the best option, as it won't be easy for them to see each other and make eye contact without straining their necks. Ideally, you'll want to arrange the chairs in a broad arc, almost forming a semicircle, so that each participant can have a clear view of the audience and the other panelists. This has a nice way of enhancing the group dynamics. Also, make sure you're positioned in a way that all panelists can see you. This is important if you need to send subtle time signals to your panelists.

Give a Quick Preview of What's to Come

At the start of the session, let your audience know how you plan to run the show. Briefly walk them through the agenda and give them a sense of how the session will be structured. Be prepared to deliver short opening remarks that frame the issues and set the agenda. Time your remarks beforehand so you don't go on for too long. Remember, you're not the main attraction. You're there to support and showcase the panelists.

Introduce the Panelists Succinctly

Keep your introductions short. You shouldn't need to spend more than thirty seconds introducing each panelist. Decide whether you want to have each panel member deliver brief opening remarks or go straight to the question-and-answer session and discussion. If panelists will be making introductory comments, set a time limit and stick to it. (You should ask panelists to time their remarks beforehand so they don't run overtime.)

Panelists often use their opening remarks as a way to promote themselves or their company. As a result, they often drone on with too much detail. So there's a case to be made for not having the panelists introduce themselves (you control the introductions as stated above) and moving right to the questions and answers. Keep in mind that audiences usually aren't all that interested in prepared remarks. Panels by their very nature are designed to encourage a lively exchange of ideas and a variety of viewpoints. This is what engages and interests everyone. So do everything you can to give them what they came for.

Be a Good Timekeeper

Presenters often have difficulty gauging how long their remarks will take when they're presenting in real time. So consider working out a system to signal panelists when their time limit is approaching. One thing you can do is simply move forward in your seat, lean in a bit, and make eye contact with the panelist who needs to wrap things up. Or if you're sitting off to the side, stand up to get their attention. If this doesn't work, you may need to become more proactive. Look for an opening to interject something like, "Bill, that's an interesting thought. Sherry, what has your experience been with this?" To ensure that your event runs smoothly and efficiently, take your watch out and use it for timing. Consider placing it in front of you on your table. This way you can discreetly check the time without turning your wrist.

Make Valuable Contributions Without Stealing the Spotlight

Good moderators know how and when to interject their thoughts to help stimulate a discussion. It's certainly possible to impart your knowledge and expertise in the way you frame a question. For example, when transitioning from one presenter to another, you might say something like, "There are some interesting trends emerging in the global economy. How do you think the appointment of a new Federal

Reserve chairman will impact interest rates in the short term and what effect, if any, will that have on the overall economy?" You can also relate elements of the discussion to a current news item. For example, "According to a recent story in the *Wall Street Journal*, one in five baby boomers will be retiring from the workforce over the next five to ten years. Experts I've spoken to have said this could have a major impact on future recruiting efforts. Do you agree and if so, what steps are you starting to take to deal with this issue?"

Handling Questions

Questions for panelists can be handled in two ways. You can hand out note cards in advance that can be collected and returned to you before the question-and-answer segment, or you can take questions directly from the floor. Sometimes a combination of both approaches works well, too. It's always a good idea to repeat the question so that everyone in the room hears it. (The panelist who is answering the question will also appreciate the extra time to formulate his or her answer.) If a question is unclear, you may want to rephrase it. If an audience member doesn't direct his or her question to a specific panelist, and instead puts it out to the entire panel, consider stepping in and directing it to the panelist who is best qualified to handle it. The last thing you want is a free-for-all, where every panel member chimes in with a response. So don't be afraid to say something like, "So that we can take as many of your questions as possible, please direct your question to one panelist. If you're not sure who to ask, I will be happy to direct your question for you." If you're running short of time and there are still more questions from the audience, you can invite audience members to talk with the panelists during a break or at the end of the session.

Don't hesitate to tell your panelists how you would like them to respond to questions. If you want them to be brief and to the point so other panelists have an opportunity to express their point of view, say so. Once again, be on the lookout for long-winded answers. It's easy for panelists to lose track of time, especially when spontaneously responding to impromptu questions.

Be an Active Listener and Take Notes

Keep a notepad nearby so you can jot down trigger words and key points that panelists say. When possible, make an effort to tie their remarks in to subsequent questions. For example, "Jim told us earlier about the court ruling that was just handed down. Rosemary, how will this affect the way you do business?" Taking notes has an added benefit: by the end of the discussion you'll have a concise outline of what all the panelists have said right in front of you. You can then incorporate these comments into your summary. By the way, when it's all over, don't forget to ask the audience to give the panelists a round of applause.

THINKING ON YOUR FEET

You're in a meeting and your manager suddenly asks for an update on the project you're working on. You're caught off guard and draw a blank. Or maybe you're part of a group sitting around a table and the person in charge unexpectedly asks each person to introduce themselves and talk briefly about what they do. You sit there in a panic and wonder what you're going to say and how it's going to sound. Or how many times have you been asked a question that you're qualified to answer, yet you struggle to get your bearings and actually blurt out something that makes you sound a lot less knowledgeable than you really are?

It's not easy being put on the spot. It's hard enough speaking in public when you're prepared, but it's ten times harder when you're not. Handling impromptu speaking situations such as the ones described above doesn't have to be a nightmare. In fact, many of the same principles that govern prepared remarks actually work well when you have to speak off the cuff. Here are a few simple guidelines that can help you think better on your feet and appear calm, collected, knowledgeable, and in control—even if you haven't had a lot of time to prepare.

Use the Power of the Pause

When asked to speak on the spur of the moment, don't jump right in. Stop to think for a moment. Make sure you have a clear understanding of what you're being asked before you respond. If you don't understand the question ask for clarification. Rephrase the question if appropriate. If it's a significant question there's nothing wrong with saying something like, "You've just asked a very important question. Let me take a moment to give that some thought." This buys you an extra few seconds, which is usually all you'll need to formulate your initial response. Remember, when you're put on the spot, do everything you can to take the pressure off yourself. You don't have to be brilliant, just coherent.

Make a Quick Outline and Keep It Simple

If you have a moment to prepare, jot down two or three bullet points on a piece of paper (use a business card or napkin if there's nothing else around). I always advise my clients to carry a few three-by-five-inch index cards just in case. But if there's no time for notes, don't panic. You won't get stuck if you keep it simple. All you need to do is start with one main point or idea and have a couple of subpoints to elaborate on it. Your supporting points can consist of an example or anecdote and that's it. You don't always need to have two or three main points to give a good response. You'll find that once you start talking other ideas may pop into your head. Try to manage the inventory of information in your brain. Filter out what's not relevant to your main idea. Don't go off on a tangent just to eat up time. This can lead you down the wrong path and you may find it difficult to get back on track. Most of all, keep in mind that for impromptu speaking you really don't need to cover too much ground.

Specific Strategies to Structure Your Thoughts

Yes, it *is* possible to structure your thoughts, even on the spur of the moment. Here are a few of the most common ways to organize ideas.

- *Chronologically*. Use a past, present, future sequence. "When we first started out . . . ," "What we're now experiencing is . . . ," "Based on current trends we expect to see . . ."
- *By listing key points*. "We're currently working on three initiatives: One . . . Two . . . Three . . ." Be aware however, that numbering your points does come with some risks. You could finish point two and then forget your last point. So, to be on the safe side, consider saying something like, "We're currently working on a

number of initiatives. I'm going to focus on A." This
gets you off the hook.

- *In a problem-cause-solution sequence.* State the problem,
explain the cause, and offer a possible solution. "The
problem we're facing is skyrocketing gasoline prices
due to soaring energy costs. We need to start thinking
about alternative sources of energy such as . . ."

- *By moving from the general to the specific.* When you're
suddenly called upon to speak, take a step back first. If
you're hit with a tough question, start by discussing the
issue rather than forcing yourself to come up with "the
right answer." Provide a little background on the situation. Begin with a general statement before getting to
the specifics. For example, "This is an issue that we've
been dealing with for some time now. We've attended a
number of off-site meetings to get a broader perspective
on this. Here's what we're starting to see . . ."

- *By giving the pros and cons.* This is a great technique
when someone unexpectedly asks your opinion about
something. The trick here is not to allow yourself to
get pinned down to an answer you don't want to give.
So if you get a question like, "What do you think about
Susan Johnson—do you think we should keep her or
let her go?" You might respond with "Let's discuss the
pros and cons. On the plus side . . ."

- *Don't let your comments unravel as you finish.* Always try
to provide some structure on the back end as you con-
clude your remarks. Consider wrapping up by returning to the main theme of the question or reinforcing
your main point. For example, "So, corporate social responsibility is really everyone's job." Of course, the
tried-and-true method of telling them what you're

going to say, saying it, then telling them what you just said never fails.

It's Not Always What You Say . . .

Remember, a good delivery can often compensate for mediocre content. So can confident body language. When speaking on the fly, it's critical to look and sound polished and poised. Don't let your voice wimp out. Project your voice forward and use plenty of vocal variety to give energy and commitment to your words. When put on the spot, many people get nervous and speak too quickly. Don't fall into this trap. Take your time and make an extra effort to speak deliberately.

Be cognizant of the visual signals you're sending. You don't want to look flustered, even if you feel that way inside. Maintain eye contact with your listeners, use gestures to support your key points, practice good posture, and don't forget to smile. Remember, nonverbal communication accounts for over 90 percent of your first impression. So even if your content isn't everything you want it to be, you can still project confidence and credibility just by the way you look and sound.

Prepare for the Unexpected

It goes without saying that advance planning can minimize your chances of being caught off guard. Surprisingly, few people do it. If you get thrown a curve at a meeting, maybe you should take some of the responsibility. After all, it's not unreasonable for your supervisor to ask how the project is coming along, is it? Before you go into a meeting, try this little exercise. Put yourself in your supervisor's shoes. Ask yourself, "If I were the boss, what would I want to know from the people in this meeting?" Always have a few discussion points ready "in your back pocket" just in case. You may not be able to predict everything, but you sure can cut down on a lot of unpleasant surprises.

And what about those spur-of-the-moment introductions referred to at the start of this section? Who says those have to be unrehearsed? If you're ever asked to say a few words about yourself, this should be a slam dunk. Because who knows more about you than you? You should have several versions of your "verbal bio" ready to go at all times—the fifteen-second edition for when the CEO steps into the elevator and asks you how things are going; the thirty-second version for those dreaded around-the-table introductions; and the sixty-second version for when you're at a party or special event. And yes, you should practice all these versions *out loud* until they are smooth and seamless.

HOW TO SAY IT

1. As a panelist you should actively listen and look for places to interject your thoughts.
2. Do a dry run of your introductory remarks and time yourself.
3. Weave two or three take-aways into your responses.
4. Keep your answers concise when responding to questions.
5. Pay attention to the points other panelists are making so you can refer back to their comments.
6. Be cognizant of the nonverbal signals you are sending. Your body language is always communicating even when you're not speaking.
7. If you're moderating a panel, you should guide and

steer the discussion, while serving as a mediator for the panelists.

8. When introducing panelists, be concise. If panelists are making introductory comments, set a time limit and stick to it.

9. Be a good timekeeper. Be on the lookout for long-winded answers and work out a system to signal panelists when their time limit is approaching.

10. If an audience member asks a question to the entire panel, step in and direct the question to the panelist who is best qualified to answer.

11. When you're asked to speak on the spur of the moment, stop to think for a second before you respond.

12. Make a quick outline to organize your thoughts. Start with one main point and have an example or anecdote to illustrate it.

13. Structure your thoughts chronologically, by listing key points, using a problem-cause-solution format, moving from the general to the specific, or giving the pros and cons. Structure your conclusion by returning to the main theme of the question.

14. Before going into a meeting, always have a few discussion points ready in your back pocket just in case.

15. Have several versions of your "verbal bio" ready to go at all times and practice them *out loud* until they are smooth and seamless.

HOW NOT TO SAY IT

1. When presenting on a panel, don't be a silent spectator or a talk hog.

2. Don't give long-winded answers, and don't ignore

what other panelists have to say, as well as the moderator.

3. Don't join a panel discussion simply to answer questions. Have a message you want to convey.

4. Don't address your comments to the moderator or fellow panel members.

5. Don't disengage when you're not speaking, and don't talk to other panelists when someone else is speaking.

6. Don't neglect your body language and don't multitask.

7. When you're the moderator, resist the temptation to answer questions and offer your opinions.

8. Don't encourage presenters to speak to each other across the table.

9. Don't underestimate the importance of the seating arrangement.

10. Don't let questions from the audience turn your session into a free-for-all, where every panel member chimes in with a response.

11. Don't forget to ask the audience to applaud at the end.

12. Don't jump right in when asked to speak on the spur of the moment.

13. Don't allow yourself to get pinned down to an answer you don't want to give, and don't get flustered if you're put on the spot.

14. Don't let your comments unravel as you finish your response.

15. Don't neglect to practice your "verbal bio" *out loud*.

7

Mastering Different Media and Technology

In today's business environment, communicating effectively requires more than just face-to-face interaction. Increasingly, in-person encounters are being replaced by voice mail, conference calls, videoconferences, video streaming (prerecorded video messages that are played back on intranet and Internet sites), live webcasts, podcasts that can be downloaded onto iPods, and other forms of electronic communication. Making a personal connection with your audience by telecommunicating requires a specific set of skills.

AUDIO ONLY: VOICE MAIL AND CONFERENCE CALLS

Presenting on the telephone has its own unique set of challenges. Because you're heard but not seen, how you sound is of paramount importance. In fact, the way you present yourself over the telephone can directly affect whether or not you will even get a follow-up face-to-face meeting. Let's examine some helpful telephone messaging techniques.

Voice Mails

The dreaded voice-mail message is only as good (or as bad) as you make it. In some corporate cultures, voice mail is used quite frequently for regular communications (e.g., companywide messages from top management). In others, it is used a lot less. Like any other form of organizational communication, the effectiveness of voice-mail messaging tends to decrease with usage. The big downside to voice mail is that when overused, many listeners tend to see them as annoying. In fact, if they are too abundant, most voice-mail messages will wind up being deleted before they're even heard. So be forewarned: voice mail should be used wisely and sparingly, and only when the content merits it. Nevertheless, if you use voice mail you should prepare carefully, and use the same attention to detail that you would accord any other presentation.

Perhaps the best way to learn good voice-mail habits is to ask yourself what you like and dislike—or positively hate— about the messages you receive. Here are some strategies to make sure the messages you leave actually get listened to.

Keep It Short and to the Point

Don't ramble. When you leave a long-winded message your listener will likely hit Delete before it's even half over. If you want others to listen to what you have to say, keep your message under a minute long (less than thirty seconds works even better), and get to the point right away. This means cutting out the fat and focusing on the essential elements of the message. The length of your message will also depend on who your audience is. As a rule, the more senior the listener, the more concise you need to be. A first-year associate may tolerate a long message but a senior-level executive won't. So if you have to update a group of junior and senior executives, consider leaving two different messages. If necessary, you can give the junior folks more details, but stay high level and stick to the main points for the senior people.

Don't Just Wing It

Make a quick outline to organize and structure your thoughts. I'm always amazed at how few people actually take the time to do this. And then they wonder why they ramble on! You don't have to write out every word, just jot down a few bullets. If the information is complex, or if the details need to be precise, you can always add a few subbullets to your outline. This whole process takes less than a minute and is well worth every second. Having a brief bullet-point outline also gives you a clear structure to follow so you'll be less inclined to wander off on tangents. At the same time, your message will also be sharper and easier to listen to. After you say your name, headline the two or three key points you want to cover. Say, "There are three issues I want to talk about: A, B, and C." If you preview the key points at the top of the message, listeners will know what to expect and they're more likely to stay on for the entire message, especially if the last item is important to them.

Determine the Tone You Want to Convey

Once your outline is in place, there's one more critical step you need to take. Remember, effective telephone

communication is as much about having the right tone and
delivery as having the right content. So take a look at the
points on your outline and ask yourself, "What tone do I
want to convey?" This really gets back to finding your actionable purpose or *intention*, which is examined in chapter 2. Do you want to excite, warn, challenge, reassure,
shake up, or entertain? Write down your intention on your
outline and make sure the tone of your voice matches your
words. In other words, use plenty of vocal variety.

Don't Get Robotic

Voice-mail messages, by their very nature, aren't exactly interactive exchanges. On the surface a voice-mail message is
a one-way form of communication spoken into a sterile
piece of telecom equipment. If you're not careful, you could
wind up sounding as mechanical as the equipment you're
using, and when that happens, it's not a pleasant listening
experience. There are many things you can do to put some
personality and pizzazz into your delivery. Start by using
plenty of vocal variety. Highlight the key words on your
bullet outline and keep your voice jumping on the most important points. Next, consider standing up when leaving
your message. Walk around a bit and gesture as you talk.
You'll be surprised at how this can energize and animate
your delivery. Finally, picture the person you're talking to.
If you've already met, visualize him or her as you're talking.
If you haven't met, put a face on your listener. Paint an image in your mind of what you think that person might look
like. The goal is to create the impression that you are actually interacting with someone, having a real dialogue (not a
disengaged monologue) where you can personally connect.

Speak Clearly and Distinctly

How many times have you listened to—or tried to listen to—a voice-mail message only to get to the very end and not be able to make out the person's name or phone number? Sometimes playing it back a second or third time doesn't help. Why? The speaker raced through so fast you can't make out the caller's name and return number. This doesn't have to happen. For starters, take your time when saying your name. Make sure you separate your first and last name (especially if you have an unusual-sounding name). Also, make an extra effort to clearly enunciate the ends of your words—when you speak too fast word endings tend to get swallowed. You can do two things to make phone numbers easy to understand from the start:

1. Subdivide your number into four distinct groups. For example, if your number is 212.555.3129, don't say it all in one breath. Instead, say 212—555—31—29.
2. Repeat your number the same way as before.

Time Your Message

If you're like most people, you probably don't realize how long the message you're leaving really is until you hear it played back. What can seem like a short message to you may wind up going way over the mark. So take out your watch and time yourself, or if your phone has a digital time display, use it. With your conversational rate of speech, do a test run *out loud* and see how long your message runs. If you're over a minute, make some cuts.

Play Back Important Messages Before You Send Them

Don't send out a message you'll regret. If you have a voice-mail system that allows you to play back your message before you send it, by all means use it! Most business systems provide a playback feature. Simply listen for the prompt. If you don't like the way you sound, you can rerecord it. If your voice-mail system doesn't have this feature, leave the message on your cell phone and play it back. As you listen, evaluate your content as well as your delivery (this is also another opportunity to time your remarks). Make sure the flow of ideas is crystal clear and that your voice tone matches your words. If you don't like what you hear, do it over again.

Finally, if you think e-mails are replacing voice-mail messages and voice mail is becoming less of a priority, think again. By being more selective with the voice-mail messages you leave, you can make them even more of a priority or special event for you and your listeners. In many e-mail cultures the new way of thinking is, "Gee, if he's leaving me a voice mail, it must really be important." In other words, there's more on the line now than ever before. Think about this the next time you pick up the phone to leave someone a message.

Conference Calls

Conference calls last substantially longer than voice-mail messages and typically involve a group of participants interacting over the telephone. This dynamic creates a new set of challenges all their own. Let's look at these issues and explore some techniques to master this medium.

Engage the Remote Callers

How can you actively involve participants who are not in the room? One surefire way is to periodically ask questions. But don't just pose a general question to the entire group. For example, don't say, "Does anyone have any comments to add?" The question is so general in nature, it can leave you with an awkward gap of silence. Instead, address your questions using specific names of participants. For example, say, "Roger, how do you envision this?" Don't underestimate the power of using names. If listeners are prone to multitasking while you're talking, referring to them by name will keep everyone on their toes. Consider keeping a call list nearby so you can refer to those on the call by name. Ask questions periodically to clarify understanding. This is especially important on the phone where you can't see the body language and facial expressions of the people you're interacting with. On the phone, silence can be misinterpreted. Don't assume that the absence of conversation means callers understand or agree with what has just been said. Always try to get feedback from individuals.

Give Everyone a Chance to Talk

Have each caller say hello and introduce themselves at the start. For larger meetings, ask participants to state their name each time before speaking. Don't be a talk hog. Do your best to make sure everyone has an opportunity to contribute. If your subordinates are on the call, let them have airtime. Chances are they have valuable information to offer. Keep track of who has spoken and who hasn't. When appropriate, try to involve the silent callers and actively manage the motormouths. If you're having a hard time making your point in a fast-paced discussion, use the "polite interruption" techniques described on pages 61–62. Be a good listener, and don't talk over people unless it's absolutely necessary.

Break the Monotony of Long Calls

If appropriate, stand up once in a while as you speak to energize yourself and your delivery. Getting the blood circulating also helps project your voice with greater clarity and authority. Walk around a bit and gesture as you speak—you'll sound more conversational and less presentational. Use plenty of vocal variety to avoid sounding flat and monotonous. Listening to one speaker dominate a long call is just plain boring, no matter how senior the person is. So make an effort to break things up and let other voices be heard. A variety of voices and viewpoints is always more interesting to listen to.

Additional Tips for Conference Calls

- Be concise. Don't waste other people's time with unnecessary comments.
- Don't shout into the speakerphone. You should be able to talk normally and still be heard. It's better to reposition yourself closer to the phone than shout from a distance.
- Be cognizant of your tone, speed, volume, and diction—these are all critical components in how you come across on the phone.
- Pay particular attention to how you emphasize key words. Use the three P's: pitch, pace, and pausing (see "Mastering Vocal Variety" on pages 135–38). You need

to be able to convey conviction on your main points throughout your delivery.

- Practice good telephone posture. Don't slouch, hunch, or lean back too far in your chair.
- If you're in a room with other participants, avoid side discussions. If you need to address a point that's off topic, use your mute button or pass along a note.
- End the call with a brief recap that drives home the key points of the meeting.
- Consider tape-recording the conference call to see how communication might be improved the next time around.

AUDIO AND VISUAL: VIDEOCONFERENCES, VIDEO STREAMING, AND WEBCASTS

Learning how to look and sound natural, confident, and convincing in nontraditional settings such as videoconferences, video-streaming messages, or webcasts poses new challenges for even the most experienced of speakers. Those who can project warmth, sincerity, and trust in these electronic formats will have a true competitive edge. What we want to achieve in these formats is the same as in any other presentation—compelling messages that get results. Let's explore the technological capabilities that these formats offer, and then look at some specific techniques that will help maximize the effectiveness of your presentations in each.

Videoconferencing, video streaming (transmitting full-motion video over the Internet), and webcasting all involve cameras, and therefore add a critical visual component to remote communication. Your posture, body language, and facial expressions are all front and center for the world to see. And when you're on camera, what you say takes a backseat to the way you look and the way you sound.

What to Wear (and What Not to Wear) for the Camera

- Avoid white shirts and white clothing, which can cause a glare on camera. (If you must wear a white shirt or blouse, wear a dark jacket over it.) Light blue or pastel colors work best.
- Avoid busy patterns such as pinstripes, herringbone patterns, small checked patterns, polka dots, etc. Wear a solid color or muted patterns instead.
- Avoid bulky clothing (it makes you appear bigger than you really are).
- Avoid big, shiny, dangling jewelry (it can cause reflections and create distracting sounds).
- Go easy with hairstyling. Simple is always best on camera.
- If makeup is offered take advantage of it. When done right, you'll appear warmer on-screen.

Videoconferences

One of the most important things to keep in mind when doing a videoconference is knowing where to focus your eyes when you're speaking. To engage remote participants, always look directly into the camera when you're talking. At the same time, resist the temptation to look at remote participants on the screen as you're speaking. This will actually turn your eyes away from your remote listeners. The only way to make direct eye contact with your audience is through the lens of the camera. If you're having trouble with this, consider posting a sticker right above the camera lens as a visual reminder of where to look.

You should only be looking at the television screen when you're listening to others speak. Keep in mind that there is a transmission delay in the audio and visual portions of the communication. If you've ever watched a TV interview with a reporter in a distant location, you've probably noticed a slight delay in his or her response time. To compensate for this time lag, make sure you speak clearly and distinctly. If you're a fast talker, you'll need to make an extra effort to slow yourself down. Also, take your time when responding to questions and comments. When you've finished speaking, pause for a second to allow others to respond. Don't interrupt or talk over other speakers as it may cause sounds to get garbled. On the visual side, try to avoid any sudden movements as they tend to blur on the screen. If you intend to walk around during your presentation, don't walk too fast.

Here are some additional pointers to keep in mind during video casts:

- Participants should identify themselves and their locations before speaking ("This is Mary from Chicago and I'd like to introduce my team").
- Have a list of names of the remote attendees and their locations next to you so you know who's who.
- Actively involve remote participants in the discussion by periodically asking open-ended questions to get their thoughts and opinions.

- Avoid fidgeting, indulgent yawning, or side conversations. Remember, you are always on camera, even when you're not speaking.
- Sit straight, and lean slightly forward into the camera.
- Keep your arms in front of you and gesture occasionally (smaller gestures work better on camera). Don't cross your hands or interlock your fingers.
- Project your voice forward and use plenty of vocal variety to highlight your key points.
- Be expressive and don't forget to smile. The more high-tech the communication, the more warmth you need to convey.

Video Streaming, Webcasts, and Other Video Presentations

High-production video presentations such as webcasts, web conferencing, and video streaming typically require special equipment and a technical crew. Extra lights are brought in, a sound engineer does the audio recording, and a director supervises the shoot. As noted in the previous section, in some cases you may even have a makeup artist on-site. By the time everything is set up, your conference room looks more like a television studio. For first-time video presenters, it can all be a bit disconcerting and overwhelming.

Your first priority is to get comfortable in your new surroundings. Determine if you'll be standing or sitting. If you're seated, make sure you're using a comfortable chair that encourages good posture. For example, you shouldn't be sitting on a sagging couch. If you're using a chair that's high off the ground (such as a director's chair), where your feet won't touch the floor, find a platform of some sort (a cardboard box will do the job) to rest your feet on. If you're standing, find a position that makes you look comfortable and relaxed. Consider having a prop to stand behind, such as a chair for resting your hands on (of course, the chair should not appear in the frame of the shot). The point to remember is this: to appear natural on camera, you have to make the time to get comfortable.

Look and Sound Natural on Camera: Don't Freeze!

Inexperienced presenters typically wear that "deer-in-the-headlights" expression when speaking to the camera. The symptoms are easy to spot: your face becomes overly serious, your body gets stiff and rigid, and your voice sounds flat and monotonous; a real talking-head robot. But it doesn't have to be. Here are a few things you can do to bring out your natural personality when the camera is on:

- Be expressive with your voice and face. Realize that you lose about 20 percent of your energy on camera compared to presenting in person. It's just the nature of the medium. So make an extra effort to modulate your voice and make sure your face matches your words.
- If you have good news to report, break into a smile and show it. The one notable exception is gestures. You don't want too many hand movements appearing in the frame of the shot, so downplay your gestures a bit when on camera. Use small movements and try to keep your hands out of the way of the camera.
- And when you look into the camera, imagine there's a person you know on the other side. You'll look and sound more natural talking to a familiar face.

Sound Conversational When Speaking from a Video Script

When it comes to reading your video script you can either read from cue cards or off a teleprompter. In a visual medium you don't want to look down at your notes when facing the camera because viewers will see more of your forehead than your face. Both cue cards and the teleprompter allow you to look directly into the camera lens as you're speaking, just like a newscaster. This creates direct eye contact between you and your viewers, which is exactly what you need to connect with your audience.

If you plan to use cue cards, use a dark marker to write your notes and remember to use very large lettering. Also, keep your sentences short and punchy, and use simple, straightforward language. If you use cue cards, have someone stand *behind* the camera and hold them up as you speak. This will make it appear as though you're looking into the camera as you read. Mark up your notes and color-code them for emphasis. For instance, underline or boldface key words that you want to highlight in your presentation. Indicate pauses with double dashes (--) or slashes (//). Rehearse your script *out loud* before you record. Always do a test run to make sure everything you've written is comfortable to say.

Master the Teleprompter

If you're a newcomer to the teleprompter, make sure you allow sufficient time to practice. Unlike stationary notes, teleprompters use scrolling text, which appear on a tiny screen much in the same way that closing credits are displayed after a movie. The speed of the scrolling text is controlled by the teleprompter operator. It's his or her job to adjust the speed to your conversational speaking tempo. So you shouldn't have to adjust to the text speed. But if you feel like you're being rushed, stop and ask the operator to adjust the speed. This can all be worked out during your run-through.

Keep in mind that the teleprompter screen is substantially smaller than a standard television screen, which means you'll only see three to four words per line on the screen (there's a limit of about twenty-five characters per line, including spaces and punctuation, using a standard teleprompter font size). It's not uncommon for one sentence to take up several lines on the screen, and you only have four to five lines of text on the screen at any time. The trick is to format your text for easy delivery. Make sure you're comfortable with the line breaks. Whenever possible, the line breaks should coordinate with your natural phrasing. So if there's a place within your text where you would naturally pause, you should break the sentence and continue your script on the next line. For example, in the sentence "Despite all our efforts, we were unable to close the deal," the line break should occur after "Despite all our efforts," and the next line should begin with "we were unable to . . ."

It's always a good idea to mark up your written notes in advance for the teleprompter operator. The operator can then enter your personal markings into the system and they'll be displayed on the screen you'll be reading from. On a teleprompter you can highlight key words by <u>underlining</u> or **bold-facing** them, using all CAPITAL LETTERS and changing the font size. But with some software, you can't use *italics*. However, you can insert directional comments into your script such as "pause," "smile," "with passion," etc. And you can also put in double dashes (- -) or slashes (//) to indicate pauses. Why bother going through all this trouble? Your markings will help you read with greater meaning, making you look and sound more natural and more committed to your message. Believe me, it's worth every minute of your time.

HOW TO SAY IT

1. Use voice mail wisely and sparingly, and only when the content merits it.

2. Time yourself to keep voice-mail messages under a minute long and get to the point right away.

3. Make a quick outline to organize your thoughts and headline your two or three main points at the top of the message.

4. Make sure the tone of your voice matches your words.

5. Walk around and gesture as you talk to energize and animate your delivery.

6. Play back important messages before you send them.

7. Engage remote participants on conference calls by periodically asking them questions. Address your questions using specific names of participants.

8. Position yourself so you are close enough to the phone and can be heard easily.

9. Be cognizant of your tone, speed, volume, and diction when speaking on the phone.

10. Sit up straight when talking on the telephone.

11. During a videoconference, always look directly into the camera when you talk.

12. For the camera, wear light blue or pastel colors and choose solid colors or muted patterns. Go with simple hairstyling.

13. Be expressive, as you'll lose about 20 percent of your energy on camera.

14. Insert directional comments into your video script such as "pause," "smile," "with passion," etc.

15. Rehearse your video script *out loud* before you record.

HOW NOT TO SAY IT

1. Don't overuse voice mail.

2. Don't ramble and leave long-winded messages, and don't sound robotic.

3. Don't just pick up the phone and leave a message without thinking about what you need to say and how you need to say it.

4. Don't race through your name and phone number when leaving a message.

5. Don't forget to time your message.

6. Don't send out a message you'll regret. Always play back important messages before you send them.

7. On conference calls, don't underestimate the power of using people's names.

8. Don't assume that the absence of conversation means callers understand or agree with what has just been said.

9. Don't talk over people unless it's absolutely necessary.

10. Don't shout into the speakerphone.
11. When videoconferencing, don't look at the television screen as you're speaking.
12. Avoid any sudden movements, fidgeting, indulgent yawning, or side conversations when videoconferencing.
13. Avoid wearing white clothing, busy patterns, and big, shiny jewelry on camera.
14. Don't think your normal energy level will work on camera.
15. Don't record until you have rehearsed your video script *out loud*, and you're comfortable in your surroundings.

8

It's Not Just the Words, It's the Delivery

Why do some speakers come across like they're just going through the motions, while others appear passionate and excited, and leave their audiences longing for more?

To understand the answer, let's go back to the introduction of this book, where I described two basic types of speakers. The first merely recites the facts in a disconnected way. The second engages audiences by inviting them to listen to a clear and powerful message. What accounts for such a stark difference?

Well, it's not just *what* these speakers say, it's *how* they say it. The right words will only get you so far. As a colleague of mine says, "Words spoken without feelings are like plastic flowers—sterile and unstirring."

There is plenty of research to back this up. One UCLA study found that the way you sound—apart from the words you use and the way you look—accounts for close to 40 percent of the meaning of your message. In fact, the same study revealed that only 7 percent of the meaning was derived from the actual content! Despite all this evidence, most pre-senters spend the bulk of their time and energy fixated on perfecting the content, while paying little or no attention to their delivery. The lesson that escapes so many is this: you can't be a persuasive presenter unless you're equally cog-nizant of both content and *delivery*.

What do you do if your delivery isn't what it should be? Let's take a look at the most common delivery problems and how to resolve them.

Ten Common Speaking Problems That Can Sabotage a Great Presentation and How to Correct Them

- **Talking Too Fast** Speaking too quickly doesn't just make what you say harder for listeners to absorb, it makes what you say sound less important. The percep-tion is if you're rushing through the information, it's not worth focusing on. Rapid-fire speech also creates a credibility problem. It conjures up images of fast-talking used car salesmen. Is that the kind of image you want to project?

  Remedy: This problem is caused when your mind races ahead of your mouth. It creates a verbal traffic jam whereby too many words are crammed into each breath, and you wind up rushing to complete every thought. Your brain and your mouth work at two very different speeds. Think of the Internet. Your brain has a high-speed connection while your mouth is on dial-up. (Which means you can't possibly speak as quickly or ef-fectively as you think.) To help the two work together, don't get too far ahead of yourself. Concentrate on one thought at a time. Break your thoughts down into smaller chunks and pause to breathe as you speak. This will make your information easier for others to digest. Think of punctuating your speech with pauses. Add commas as you talk. Pause for punctuation—commas, periods, paragraph breaks—page turns, and whenever you're listing a series of items. This will slow your pace. Even the shortest pauses can be very powerful. So don't be afraid to take a moment of silence. Your listeners need a second of silence to absorb what you've just said, so pauses benefit both you and your audience. You can also write "slow down" or "pause" in your notes or outline or by your telephone as a visual reminder. Remember, your work pace may be hectic, but your rate of speech shouldn't.

- **Slow, Halting Speech** Most of the people I work with talk too fast. But talking too slowly can be just as frustrating for listeners as talking too fast. Think about it from the audience's perspective—waiting for your next word to come along can really annoy listeners and make them impatient. It's a lot like being stuck behind a very slow driver on a winding two-lane road. Some people will assume that if you talk slowly you're also a slow thinker. In other words, you may be perceived as not very bright. So if you're a slow talker you'll need to adjust your speedometer.

    Remedy: Pick up the pace. Try to bring your speed in line with those you're talking to. Here's where it pays to know your audience. If you're speaking to a group of New Yorkers, who tend to talk more rapidly than those in other regions, don't be afraid to accelerate your pace. Also, make sure your voice is well modulated. Adding color and variety to your delivery can make a slow pace more interesting to listen to.

• **Mumbling** Your mother was right when she said, "Don't mumble!" If your words run together and are hard to make out, you're putting an extra burden on others to understand you. Remember when Jesse Jackson first hit the scene? Despite being a well-respected and passionate speaker, his habit of mumbling and slurring words made him difficult to understand. He was perceived by some to be less polished because of his sloppy speech. Mumbling can also make you appear less than forthcoming. Indistinct speech can create the perception that you may be trying to hide something. People mumble when they close their mouths too much and speak with a voice that is too low. It sounds sloppy and lazy. The impression is if you're sloppy or lazy in your speech, you may be sloppy or lazy in other ways as well.

Remedy: Open your mouth wider when you speak and don't swallow your words. Keep your voice strong from start to finish. Enunciate your words clearly and distinctly. Avoid talking with your hand in front of your mouth. Tape-record yourself and check to see if you're dropping certain sounds and syllables. Make an extra effort to pronounce the ends of your words. Practice diction drills to exercise the muscles in your mouth and improve your articulation. (My previous book, *How to Say It with Your Voice*, gives more information on getting rid of sloppy speech.)

• **Mispronunciations** Do you say "reconize" when you mean "recognize"? Does "picture" sound like "pitcher"?

We all mispronounce a word now and then. But if you have a habit of mispronouncing *common* words, this can turn into a problem. It can make you sound less intelligent. President Bush's mispronunciations, or "Bushisms," certainly has given late-night comedians ample material to have fun with. Take the word "nuclear." Instead of saying the standard American pronunciation, "new-klee-ur," Bush says "new-cue-lur." According to insiders, Bush thinks his version sounds "folksy" and endears him to the public. This can easily backfire. Even some of his strong supporters have been known to roll their eyes and smirk when Bush repeatedly mispronounces common words. "Folksy and endearing"? I don't think so. Like it or not, standard American pronunciation is what the majority of well-educated people in this country use.

Remedy: One of the best ways to check if you're saying your words correctly is to consult a dictionary. Look at the pronunciation guide next to the word and see how this compares to the way you say it. Also, listen to the way well-educated speakers say their words. To hear standard American pronunciation in action, watch or listen to any national news program.

- **Bad Grammar** Grammar bloopers can make you sound unprofessional and incompetent. Keep in mind that people often base their opinions about you on your command of the English language. So it's vitally important to pay attention to the words you select and how you put them together. They can make or break your image.

  Remedy: You don't need to memorize a laundry list of complex rules and confusing terminology, just focus on the most common mistakes or bloopers to prevent any embarrassing situations. (For a quick grammar refresher see my previous book, *How to Say It with Your Voice*.)

- **Overuse of "Ums" and "Ahs"** Do you salt your speech with fillers such as "you know," "okay," "like," and "uh"? While the occasional "um" or "you know" isn't the end of the world, excessive use of fillers weakens your message and can distract your listeners.

  Remedy: How frequently do junk words pop up in your speech? Have someone keep count when you make your next presentation. Or record yourself during a series of telephone conversations at home or at work. Play back the tape and start counting the "ums" and "ahs" and other unwanted fillers in your speech. The numbers may surprise you. But don't panic. Replace these fillers with brief pauses. There's no need to "verbalize" these pauses with junk words. Use visual aids. Jot down your most common fillers on a sticker and post it on or by your telephone. Each time you talk on the phone, you'll have a visual reminder of what not to say. If you're giving a presentation, write down your favorite filler(s) on the pages of your presentation book or in your notes.

- **Up-Speak** When you make a statement, does it sound like you're asking a question? Does your voice rise in pitch at the end of a sentence—even if you're not asking a question? This is called "up-speak," a condition where what you say is being undercut but how you say it. If your voice goes up as you end your statement, you're taking the authority and conviction right out of your message. It makes you sound weak and tentative.

  Remedy: Drop your voice down in pitch when you come to the final word of your statement. Think of ending your statement with an exclamation point! It's the difference between sounding sure or insecure. If you suffer from up-speak, it's often hard to catch yourself in the act as you are speaking. Again, the answer here is to record yourself whenever possible. Monitor your inflection pattern and make sure the pitch of your voice drops down at the end of declarative statements.

- **Trailing Off at the Ends of Sentences** Ever hear a speaker who starts off well and then dies out at the end of the sentence? It's like someone has pulled the plug out. This makes the last few words difficult to hear, which can weaken the message and sometimes even kill an entire thought. What causes this? Sometimes people lose steam at the end because they cram too many words into each breath and run out of air prematurely. Discarding the end of a thought also happens when your mind is already on to your next thought before you have finished saying your current one.

  Remedy: Concentrate on one thought at a time, and make an effort to keep the sound of your voice strong until the very end of your sentence. Your last few words are often the most important in terms of audience recall so it would be a real shame to lose out on an important opportunity to connect with listeners.

- **Weak Qualifiers** Too often I hear people use qualifying expressions such as "I pretty much think . . . ," "I believe . . . ," "Hopefully, we'll be able to . . . ," "You may disagree with this but . . . ," "Maybe we can . . . ," and "I guess . . ." Weak qualifiers like these prevent you from making a strong, clear, and direct response or statement. They preface your message with doubt and uncertainty, and can dilute the conviction that you bring to the table.

Remedy: Take the qualifiers out and put the confidence and conviction back in. Just get to the point. Instead of saying, "I believe our company has the best research team in the business," simply say, "Our company has the best research team in the business." This sounds a lot stronger and more convincing. If you truly believe in what you're saying you don't need to utter the word "believe." It just goes without saying. Instead of saying "Hopefully, we'll be able to . . . ," say "We're confident we'll be able to . . ." Don't worry about coming on too strong. It sure beats sounding apologetic for no reason.

- **Overused Words and Phrases** If trendy buzzwords such as "paradigm," "synergy," "value-added," "robust," and "value proposition" are mainstays of your vocabulary, it's time to look for some alternatives. When overdone, these terms actually lose their impact and can annoy listeners. Also, watch out for industry jargon. Know who you are talking to. Speaking to an external audience often requires different language and vocabulary than internal audiences. Many organizations have their own internal lingo (including acronyms) that are used all the time around the office. These coded expressions have a limited external shelf life and can often leave outsiders in the dark.

Remedy: Consult a dictionary or thesaurus to find good alternatives to overused buzzwords. Don't overdose on acronyms and industry jargon. Use words everyone can understand. If you need to use a technical term, define it for your audience. If an acronym slips out, tell your audience what it stands for.

There's one more common speaking problem that's so important it deserves its own special section. I'm talking about the flat, monotonous delivery. Read on.

PROJECTING PASSION, ENERGY, AND COMMITMENT

Have you ever been in a meeting where someone else says pretty much the same thing you just said but gets all the credit for it? It hurts and it's not fair. But it happens all the time. Another person delivers the same thought with more passion and punch and gets the glory. It underscores how important the delivery (i.e., how you sound) is to your presentation.

Lose the "executive-speak." The problem is many professionals leave their personalities at the door when they arrive at the office. While it's true that the business environment requires you to exercise a certain level of emotional restraint, some people take it too far. They equate an executive presence with being reserved, and when it comes time to present, all their energy, passion, and commitment go right out the door. The end product is a speech or presentation that is flat and lifeless. Their voices become devoid of enthusiasm and excitement. Many business presenters may believe in what they're saying but they don't sound the least bit committed to their message. You can't energize other people and get them committed to your cause without projecting your own energy and commitment. Even the best-organized presentation won't stand a chance.

Different speakers have different energy levels. There are low-energy, moderate-energy, and high-energy speakers. Think of an energy scale from 1 to 10. Low-energy speakers range from 1 to 3; moderate-energy speakers range from 4 to 7; and high-energy speakers range from 8 to 10. Most people I work with range from 2 to 7. Remember, your energy level directly corresponds to how others perceive your level of commitment.

Low-energy speakers are flat and monotonous. Their voices have very little color and variety, and their delivery is almost robotic. Think of former Federal Reserve chairman Alan Greenspan. He's not what I would call a captivating speaker. People pay attention to him because of the position he once held. But most Level 1 speakers don't have that luxury. Audiences won't stay tuned in very long, and they certainly aren't going to remember much of what was said.

Moderate-energy speakers are neither boring nor captivating. They're sort of middle of the road, and usually that's how they are remembered. At best, they're a glass half full. Moderate-energy speakers have some color and variety, but always within a very tight range. They generally don't do a great job of highlighting key message points. And they bring no real passion, excitement, or enthusiasm to the table. Audiences will pay attention some of the time and tune out some of the time. Do they remember much? Not likely.

High-energy speakers grab and hold your attention throughout a presentation. They sound excited about what they're saying and project a strong commitment to their message. Their passion is contagious. Audiences are naturally drawn to them and enjoy listening. High-energy speakers almost always have high-energy voices, featuring plenty of color and variety. Key message points are highlighted well and listener retention is high. High-energy speakers can also motivate people to act.

So what sets high-energy speakers apart from the crowd? It's how they use their voices. Let's examine the primary elements of great vocal orchestration.

Mastering Vocal Variety

To be a powerful, credible, and dynamic speaker you need to practice and master three key elements of vocal variety. Think of these as the three P's: pitch, pace, and pausing.

1. Pitch

Captivating speakers use a lot of vocal modulation or pitch change. Their voices move up and down using a wide range of "notes." The voice jumps way up on important words to highlight them. If you're not a high-energy speaker these jumps are going to feel much bigger than you're used to. So to get the full effect, you really need to exaggerate this up and down movement. You may feel silly as you go through this, but that's okay. To distinguish between what this dramatic pitch change *feels* like to you versus what it *sounds* like to others, tape-record your practice sessions and listen carefully. You have to hear it to believe it.

Dramatically change the pitch of your voice on the italicized word(s) below:

There has been a *dramatic* increase in productivity.
Over *twenty-five* percent of our sales force has set *record* numbers.

We have a good strategy; now we need to *execute* it!
This is a time of *unprecedented* risks.

TIP: Your voice should jump the highest on the most important words of your message—the words that best help to convey your point. Modulate your voice on qualifying or descriptive words, such as adjectives and adverbs. Action verbs work well, too.

2. Pace

Pace refers to speed or tempo. Effective speakers vary their speed according to the significance of their thoughts. When something is really important they take extra time to drive it home. Slowing down on key words and phrases gives them more weight and makes key points more memorable. Think of your key points as main attractions. You wouldn't want to speed through a tour and miss out on the major sights, would you? Yet this is precisely what many speakers do. They barrel through all their points regardless of their importance, causing listeners to miss important information.

Take extra time to stretch out and emphasize the hyphenated words:

The president had an *a-m-a-z-i-n-g* opportunity.
She saw a *s-i-g-n-i-f-i-c-a-n-t* difference in the numbers.
We now have a *t-h-i-r-t-y–t-h-r-e-e* percent market share.

3. Pausing

As noted earlier in this chapter, even the tiniest pauses can pack a lot of power. Just as moments of silence or rest create drama in music (think of the opening of Beethoven's Fifth Symphony), pausing when we speak can have the same kind of dramatic effect. Look carefully at the pauses in the memorable passages below from Neil Armstrong and John F. Kennedy.

> *"One small step for man—one giant leap for mankind."*
> —Neil Armstrong

> *"Ask not what your country can do for you—ask what you can do for your country."*   —JFK

Clearly, the pauses in these examples add power and drama. But even a second or two of silence in the middle of a thought can feel like an eternity for many speakers. In fact, some will cheat the pause and substitute junk words like "um" or "uh." This kills the whole point of pausing. Resist the temptation to fill the airwaves with sound. When used well, pauses can hold the attention of your audience. They can draw listeners in and increase their curiosity. This all happens in a second or two, but it can be very powerful.

Read the following sentences aloud, stopping for the pauses as marked:

Staying on top has never been easy—but today it's tougher than ever.

Make no mistake about it—we will dominate the market.

If we get this right—we will have a very bright future.

TIP: Mark up your text or notes to indicate which words you want to emphasize and how you want to emphasize them. You should:

- Underline the key words of your presentation with a colored marker to remind you which words need a dramatic pitch change.
- Hyphenate or boldface each word you want to stretch out and take extra time on. You can even consider using a larger font size for these words.
- Write in double slashes (//) or dashes (--) to signify pauses.
- Once you've marked up your notes, go back and read your presentation out loud. Tape-record yourself to monitor your speech pattern and make sure your delivery matches your markings. Keep in mind that pitch, pace, and pausing often work together simultaneously.

Dealing with Delivery Killers

Laundry lists can be delivery killers for many presenters. No matter what they do, each item comes out sounding the same, making it difficult for listeners to remember what came before or after. The longer the list, the worse it gets. Changing the pitch of your voice on each item will help. In other words, as you describe each item you should move to a different "note" on the scale.

Modulate your voice on each of the italicized terms:

> We need *expert knowledge, strong analytical skills, talent,* and *motivation* to win this account.

Reciting Numbers

Numbers can sound extremely dry and dull if they're not handled properly. Yet numbers often tell an important story so they need to stand out. To effectively compare and contrast numbers and figures, change the pitch of your voice on each number. Look for comparative phrases—such as "in contrast to," "compared with," and "versus"—that will alert you when to modulate your voice on key figures.

> We had a *sixteen* percent increase in profit this year compared to *three* percent last year.
>
> Over the past two years, we opened *thirty* new stores versus our competitors, who opened *twelve*.

Repeated Presentations

If you're giving the same presentation over and over again, your delivery can become stale. The solution to a boring routine is to shake things up a bit. From a content standpoint, think of some new examples and anecdotes you can add to freshen up your material. On the delivery side, keep your voice jumping. As the saying goes, "you have to fake it till you make it." So if *what* you're saying isn't exciting to you, concentrate on *how* you're saying it. Using lots of inflection is a great way to make your presentation sound fresh and spontaneous. Force some passion into your delivery and the feeling will follow. You're audience will be energized. And even though you've delivered the presentation hundreds of times no one will ever know.

Technical Information

The drier and more technical your content is, the more vocal variety you'll need. Remember, just because it's dull doesn't mean it can't be brought to life. Adding interesting anecdotes, analogies, and personal examples certainly helps, but the tone of your voice makes a big difference as well. Never blame your subject matter for your boring presentation. No matter how dry the material may seem, it's your job as a speaker to give it some punch!

When You're Tired

Let's face it, going to work tired is a fact of life. Sounding tired at work is another story. The same can be said for presenting—appearing tired when you're talking is a big no-no. When you're run down, your overall energy level drops. If you're not careful, so will the energy level of your delivery. Nobody wants to listen to a flat and lifeless presenter. Keeping the bounce in your voice is a great way to hide your fatigue. If you're tired, it should be your secret.

An Unresponsive Audience

Many presenters tell me they do best when they have a captive audience. They feed off the positive energy in the room and this, in turn, energizes them. But what happens when you have an unresponsive audience? Some speakers who are not getting the enthusiastic response they hoped for just shrug it off. They go on automatic pilot, covering all the points, and leave. But that's the lazy way out. As a presenter, it's your job to set the energy level for the room. If you put no energy in, you get no energy back. Deliver a compelling presentation and your audience will respond.

Practicing Your Dynamic Delivery

Reading aloud is one of the best ways to practice your delivery skills. Here are a few things you can do:

- Read the Letters to the Editor section of your newspaper aloud. These are filled with strong opinions, which will allow you to bring out your passion and emotion. Pretend you're the writer and try to infuse your delivery with the passion and conviction that's been poured into the letter. The goal is to bring authentic energy and commitment to the words.

- Read children's stories. Children's books have lots of colorful and descriptive language. Try to paint a picture with your voice that brings the characters and images to life. Be theatrical. Use your voice to act it out! If you have kids or relatives with small children, they'll love you for it!

- Read aloud advertisements in magazines and newspapers. Imagine you're doing a commercial. Many ads are created to sell products and services so here's your chance to deliver a persuasive message.

HOW TO SAY IT

1. To control rapid-fire speech, break your thoughts down into small chunks and pause to breathe as you speak.
2. Don't swallow your words.
3. Aim for standard American pronunciation.
4. Correct common grammar mistakes.
5. Replace "ums" and "uhs" and other fillers with a split-second pause.
6. Drop your voice down in pitch on the final word of your statements.
7. Keep your voice strong through the ends of your sentences.
8. Use appropriate language and vocabulary to suit your audience.
9. Be a high-energy speaker.

10. To add vocal variety, use the 3 P's—pitch, pace, and pausing.
11. Modulate your voice when highlighting a series of items, comparing and contrasting numbers, making repeated presentations, and presenting technical information.
12. Read aloud and put some passion in your voice.

HOW NOT TO SAY IT

1. Don't speak too quickly. It can make what you say sound less important and erode your credibility.
2. Don't mumble; it sounds sloppy and lazy.
3. Avoid mispronouncing common words. It can make you sound less intelligent than you really are.
4. Avoid bad grammar; it can tarnish your image.
5. Don't overuse "ums" and "uhs"; it weakens your message.
6. Don't let your pitch rise at the end of a statement.
7. Don't trail off at the end of your thought.
8. Avoid weak qualifiers.
9. Don't overdose on acronyms and industry jargon.
10. Lose the "executive-speak."
11. Don't be a low-energy speaker.
12. Don't barrel through all your points regardless of their importance.
13. Don't neglect the power of the pause.
14. Don't get flat when you have to present numbers or technical information or make repeated presentations.

9

Building Your Voice and Body Language

Your voice is your primary business communication tool. It literally speaks volumes about who you are, and it determines how the world hears and sees you. How you use it can mean the difference between success and failure. Your voice can get you hired—or fired. It can win—or lose—a big sale. It can inspire confidence and assurance, or it can generate doubt and anxiety. Yet as important as your voice is, it receives almost no attention. And, all too often, it becomes a self-destructive liability. The same is true of body language. Your posture, gestures, facial expressions, and eye contact all send out important signals. But make sure you send the right signals. Your body language should work hand in hand with your message. The right gesture will emphasize your point. However, weak or stiff body language can weaken your message and erode your credibility.

IS YOUR VOICE SAYING THE WRONG THINGS ABOUT YOU?

Do you have a voice that moves people? Or does the mere sound of your voice make people want to move away? Believe it or not, it does matter. I once hired a leading independent research company to conduct a nationwide survey in which one thousand men and women were asked the following question: "Which irritating or unpleasant voice annoys you the most?" Heading the list were the following categories: nasal or whiny voices; high-pitched, squeaky voices; voices that are loud and grating; voices that are weak and wimpy.

- **Nasal or Whiny Voice: Chronic Complainer** Not surprisingly, the nasal or whiny tone category topped the list of most annoying voices. Let's face it, nobody likes to hear a whiner. What's the perception? You guessed it. Whiners are viewed as chronic complainers.

  Remedy: Many people tell me they think their voice sounds nasal when listening to themselves on a recording—either taped or on a voice-mail system. If that's the case here are some things you can do to address it. When the muscles in your mouth and throat become tense and constricted, you tend to speak more through your nose. Open your mouth wider and relax the throat muscles when you speak. Watch out for words with the "ow" sound (as in "down") as well as words with the short "a" sound (as in "ham"). Words like these often come out sounding very nasal.

- **High-Pitched, Squeaky Voice: Airhead** High, shrill voices can be a pain in the ear and can make you come across as flighty and frivolous. They can also make you sound immature. There are a variety of reasons for this—some people claim their voices jump a full octave whenever they get excited or tense. Whatever the cause, if you want others to take you seriously, you need to lower your pitch.

Remedy: Don't force your voice down unnaturally, as it can actually damage your vocal cords over time. It also can sound "put on." The real answer here is to relax your throat muscles as you speak and concentrate on feeling resonance or vibrating sensations in your upper chest. To learn how to expand your vocal range, see the "The Twelve-Minute Vocal Workout" section that follows.

- **Loud and Grating Voice: Bigmouth** When you open your mouth to speak, are you talking or shouting? If you've been asked to lower your voice repeatedly, you may be a loudmouth. So turn the volume down. Just like a blasting radio or TV, loud, raspy voices can really grate on people's nerves. And taken to an extreme, it can also unhinge people in meetings or presentations. Consider your audience. How will they react to you if they feel like they're sitting directly in front of a giant speaker at a rock concert? The same holds true when talking on a cell phone. The whole world doesn't need to hear your conversation.

Remedy: Ease up a bit; don't be too forceful. Practice speaking in a lower tone. Don't overcompensate and lose your entire personality. We've looked at this before. The trick is to tone it down without killing your enthusiasm or passion. (Your audience will sense this as well.) And when you're talking on a cell phone, try cupping your hand over your mouth as you speak. Chances are your listener will hear you just fine.

- **Weak and Wimpy Voice: Doormat** When speaking on the telephone, does the sound of your voice make you seem less mature and less experienced than you really are? Are you constantly interrupted or do others talk over you in meetings? Are you often asked to speak louder? Do people crane their necks to hear you? If so, you may be suffering from a weak and thin voice. You may find it hard to get respect, especially when you're competing with others who have stronger, more powerful voices.

  Remedy: For techniques to add power and authority to your voice, see "The Twelve-Minute Vocal Workout" section that follows.

ADDING POWER AND AUTHORITY TO YOUR VOICE

The Twelve-Minute Vocal Workout

Can you actually change the sound of your voice and still sound natural? You bet. Just as physical exercise can make your body stronger, there are simple exercises that can give you a deeper, richer, more resonant voice. Think of these exercises as the "calisthenics" of voice training. Famous actors and singers use these same techniques to develop their speaking voices for the stage and screen. You can practice these exercises in the shower, while getting dressed, driving in your car, or even walking. On those really hectic days when you can't find a twelve-minute block of time, try several mini workouts throughout the day. As with any exercise routine, you need to practice on a regular basis to really get results. But if you stick with it, you'll definitely notice the difference.

1. **Breathing/Relaxation Exercises for Better Breath Control (1 minute)**

   a. Aim for a long, even-flowing stream of air.

   b. Breathe normally.

   c. Open your mouth wide and keep the mouth, throat, and jaw relaxed. (Think of the mouth position you use when the doctor examines your throat.)

   d. Using the breath only (like a whisper), slowly exhale on PAH-H-H-H-H-H-H-H-H-H. (Pause.)

   e. Now slowly exhale on TAH-H-H-H-H-H-H-H-H-H.

   f. Now slowly exhale on KAH-H-H-H-H-H-H-H-H-H.

   g. Finally, slowly exhale on MAH-H-H-H-H-H-H.

2. **Hum for Resonance (3–4 minutes)** Humming is the quickest and easiest way to build power and resonance into your voice.

   a. With lips together, and breathing normally, make a long humming sound: mmmmmmmmmmmmmmm.

   b. As you hum, be aware of any buzzing or vibrating sensations in the lips, nose, and throat, as well as your upper chest. These are signs of *resonance*. Think of them as the buzzing sounds made by bumblebees, vacuum cleaners, outboard motors, electric shavers, or purring cats. The more buzz you can hear and feel, the better.

   c. Do a series of humming sounds going up and down your voice range. Start on a low note or pitch. Note by note (pausing for a little breath between each humming sound), work your way up the range, then come down again. (If you're having trouble moving your voice up and down, just hum a variety of sounds; the sequence doesn't really matter.)

   d. Concentrate on feeling the resonance. Humming is also a great way to warm up your voice. Make a few short humming sounds before you speak to assure a strong start.

3. **Strengthen Those Vowels (4–6 minutes)** Think of a vowel as a "storage unit" for sound. Practicing vowel sounds brings out the resonance in your voice and gives it more carrying power. If you're like most people, you probably don't open your mouth wide enough when you speak. This can cut your sound in half. Doing vowel-stretching exercises opens up and strengthens your voice.

   Start with the "mAH" exercise for 2–3 minutes:

   a. Hum, and open into a long "AH" sound. Let the hum lead directly into the vowel sound. The aim is to carry the humming resonance into the vowel sound. You want to make this sound vibrate or resonate.

   b. Breathing normally, hum and open up: mmmmmmmmmmmmmmmAH-H-H-H-H-H-H-H-H.

   c. Do a series of long "mAH" sounds going up and down your voice range. Start on a low note or pitch. Note by note, work your way up the range, then come down again.

   d. Concentrate on feeling resonance in the head, throat, and upper chest as you hum and open on the vowel.

   e. Listen for the "ring" and echo in your voice. This reverberation is a sure sign of richness and resonance.

   Now do the double "mAH" exercise for 2–3 minutes:

   • Do two long "mAH" sounds in each breath.

   • Follow the instructions for the previous exercise.

4. **Practice Words and Sentences (2–3 minutes)** Now it's time to take the power you've gained from the vocalizing techniques and apply it to your speech.

The following words and phrases are designed to exercise different vowel combinations. Doing a few minutes of these practice words and sentences will strengthen your speaking voice and make it more resonant.

a. Practice each word separately, saying one word in each breath.

b. Modulate your voice on each word.

c. Concentrate on feeling resonance and aim for a rich, clear sound.

d. Using your full voice, elongate each word, emphasizing the vowel sounds. For example, "agenda" should sound like "a-g-e-n-da." (Accent the stressed syllable in each word just as you would do in ordinary speech.)

agenda	ego	jovial	pacify
align	enjoy	juvenile	phobia
Amazon	epitomize	kimono	qualify
avail	fly	know-how	Siamese
avow	folio	kowtow	skyline
below	fiasco	leeway	socialize
bonanza	galvanize	liaison	tapioca
bungalow	Geneva	lullaby	tombstone
byline	geology	magnolia	Taiwan
catalogue	holiday	medallion	unify
Chicago	humanize	monotone	utilize
coincide	hallelujah	Nevada	valentine
decoy	idolize	nylon	vandalize
deny	insomnia	Oklahoma	vaudeville
dialogue	Iowa	online	Wyoming
downsize	Javanese	ozone	Yugoslavia

We need to *align* the *agenda*.
Send the *catalogue* to *Chicago*.
Don't *deny* the *dialogue*.
Our *holiday* was a *fiasco*.
I *idolize* the people of *Iowa*.
Isaiah has *insomnia*.
They have the *know-how* in *Nevada*.
She has a *phobia* about being *online*.
There's no *ozone* in *Wyoming*.

Read Aloud

Now that we've got our exercise routine in place, let's not stop here. There's plenty more you can do to enhance your vocal skills. For instance, you should be spending a few minutes every day reading out loud. As noted earlier, just about any material will do. Try poems, novels, short stories, children's stories, or plays. Newspaper and magazine articles (especially editorials and advertisements) work nicely, too. Focus on feeling resonance as you move from phrase to phrase and aim for a clear, rich sound. Modulate your voice on important words that should be read with meaning.

Speak with a Rich, Resonant Voice at Work

Be cognizant of your voice on the job. Don't fall back into your old habits. Make a conscious effort to apply what you've learned to your everyday speech. Make sure your voice is saying the right things about you regardless of whether you're on the phone, in a meeting, making a presentation, at lunch, or even chatting with someone in the hallway. For more information on how to add power and authority to your voice, see my book *How To Say It with Your Voice*.

Put an End to Voice Strain

You're not going to have an easy time commanding attention and respect if you sound hoarse. If your job requires you to raise your voice or talk for long periods of time, even on the phone, you could run into some trouble. Unfortunately, many speakers misuse their voices and end up actually hurting their vocal cords. That's the last thing any speaker wants to do. Learn how to use your voice correctly now and you'll avoid bigger problems later. Here are some of the most common causes of voice strain, along with ways to handle them.

Speaking in Noisy Surroundings

Crowded restaurants, loud parties, noisy offices, airplanes, and even air conditioners can make it difficult to judge the carrying power of your voice. Many people overcompensate by shouting. But the more you shout, the more you strain, and the less sound you get in return. If you have to speak under adverse conditions, get as close to your listener as you can and speak normally (or as close to normal as you can). Concentrate on feeling resonance in your head and chest.

Keep in mind that your ears aren't the only mechanism for judging sound. Just because you may not be able to hear your own voice, it doesn't necessarily mean you're not projecting. No matter what the external conditions may be, you can always trust the "inner feel"—the resonance vibrations—of your voice. If you feel the resonance there's no need to push any further.

Speaking Too Loudly

High-strung, aggressive speakers who force their deliveries often wind up shouting at their audiences. This can hurt your vocal cords, as well as your listeners' ears. (This shouldn't come as a surprise—very loud voices tend to grate on people's nerves.) If you suffer from frequent sore throats or you're hoarse after speaking, chances are you're overdoing it. The remedy is simple: tone it down a bit; save your voice and your listeners' ears. In this case, less is more.

Straining for a Deeper Voice

Many speakers, especially women, try to lower the pitch of their voices to sound more authoritative. In theory, this may sound like a quick fix, but it's really not. Forcing the voice down unnaturally for any length of time strains the throat muscles and can actually make you hoarse. It sounds phony, too, and listeners can sense it. The good news is you can develop a deeper, richer voice with regular exercise using the Twelve-Minute Vocal Workout earlier in this chapter. Keep in mind that a richer, more resonant voice will sound deeper without actually being lower in pitch.

Harmful Irritants

Inhaling cigarette smoke and consuming excessive amounts of liquor are not only hazardous to your health, they can also damage your voice. For example, did you know that heavy smokers and drinkers are more prone to chronic laryngitis than those who don't smoke and drink? Smoking shortens your breathing capacity, limits your vocal range, and can make you sound rough and raspy. Clearing your throat constantly can also irritate your vocal cords, and it's also very irritating to listeners. It's annoying to be in the middle of a conversation and hear a loud, scratchy *grrrrumph,* as it can really disrupt the flow of your ideas. So the next time you feel the urge to clear your throat, resist and swallow instead. Also, be aware that certain phlegm-producing foods can clog your throat. If you're about to speak, you may want to think twice before consuming a lot of dairy products like milk, cheese, or chocolate. You'll have fewer interruptions this way.

What to Do if You're Losing Your Voice

Laryngitis can be brought on by a variety of factors, including viruses, excessive talking, or heavy smoking and drinking. Resting your voice is usually the most effective cure. In most cases, you should have your full voice back within a few days. If your laryngitis persists for more than two or three days, or you suffer from a persistent sore throat or hoarseness, you should see a doctor. What can you do to prevent laryngitis from getting worse? Obviously, the best solution would be not to speak at all. But, if you must talk, use your voice sparingly. Contrary to what you may think, whispering is not always the best strategy. Some throat specialists believe that whispering can actually strain your vocal cords. So, regardless of what kind of sound comes out, try to speak normally. For sore throats, drink warm liquids such as tea and honey. Throat lozenges can be soothing, as well. Inhaling steam is also helpful. Try to avoid decongestants and antihistamines, as they tend to dry out your throat. A dry throat tends to be more prone to infection, so drink plenty of nonalcoholic and noncaffeinated fluids. Remember, developing good voice habits can help prevent throat problems in the first place.

USING BODY LANGUAGE TO REINFORCE YOUR MESSAGE

Despite what you may think, body language is not a superficial issue. It sends a very strong message. In fact, according to certain studies, over 50 percent of the meaning of your message comes from your body language and facial expressions. I've seen many presentations torpedoed by weak body language. So what body language danger signals should you be on guard for when presenting?

Posture Pitfalls

- *Leaning Too Far Back in Your Chair* Do this and you risk coming off as being a bit too casual and relaxed for many business situations. Leaning back with your hands behind your head can also make you appear arrogant, like you think you know it all. Leaning too far back in your chair can also make you appear disengaged and detached. Sit up straight and lean in slightly toward your audience.

- *Hunching Over, Slouching* Don't hunch. If your head is down and your shoulders are forward you're going to look closed in and cramped. Sit up straight, bring your shoulders back, and use an open body posture. Be careful not to slouch. Drooping shoulders can also send the wrong message. Posture that's too relaxed and casual can make you appear lazy, sloppy, or careless.

- *Swiveling in Your Chair* Many people aren't aware that they're swiveling back and forth in their chair. Yet it's distracting to watch someone rock back and forth, and it makes you look unsteady. If you're in a chair that swivels, sit at the edge of the seat. This makes it harder to rock back and forth. Plant yourself in your chair and sit still.

- *Hiding Your Hands* Don't speak with your hands under the table if you're doing a sit-down presentation. This can cause your shoulders to hunch over, making you appear closed in and cramped. Keep your arms in front of you and gesture freely as you talk. The same rule applies if you're doing a stand-up presentation. Don't clasp your hands in back of you; keep your arms out front and use big, broad gestures.

- *Being Too Relaxed while on the Telephone* Be mindful of how you sit when talking on the telephone. When you're heard and not seen, it's easy to get a little too relaxed and careless in your chair. People may not be able to see you, but lazy and sloppy posture often translates into lazy and sloppy speaking. If you spend a lot of time on the phone each day, consider standing up from time to time while you talk. It can break the seated monotony. You can even walk around a bit. This allows you to use more of your body as you speak, and can really energize your delivery.

A Few Simple Rules to Follow

- Stand or sit up straight but not rigid.
- Position your feet so your body is well balanced.
- Open and relax your shoulders.

Gestures: Think Big and Broadly

Research shows that moving your hands as you speak can actually help you think better. Don't restrict yourself by thinking that you must keep your hands down or at your sides. While it's true that too many gestures can be distracting, I usually see just the opposite problem. Many people clasp their hands tightly or fold their hands with interlocking fingers, similar to the "sit at attention" position your teacher made you do in grade school. This may have worked then, but in business it comes off looking stiff and rigid. Some presenters tend to use very limited movements when they speak. They keep their hands on the table and gesture only with their wrists, making very small movements. Using big, broad gestures helps animate your delivery. I once watched a live radio broadcaster in action as he was giving a business update. I was amazed at how many gestures he used and how expansive his movements were. When I asked him why he was so free with his gestures (this was radio after all, not TV), he said the movements reinforced his main points.

Regardless of where you are, gestures can help you express yourself more naturally. They can also give you a stronger physical presence. To help you find natural, comfortable movements, observe how you gesture the next time you chat with a friend or have a casual conversation with a colleague. Try to incorporate these "natural" movements into your business speaking. What should you do with your hands when you're not gesturing? You need to find a comfortable resting position, a good "home base." Try placing your hands one against the other by your waist with just your fingertips touching. Separate your palms and round your fingers so it doesn't look like you're praying. Since the tips of your fingers are lightly touching each other (not interlocking), you'll be able to gesture freely.

Moving with a Purpose

How should you move when you stand up to speak? You don't want to stay in one place the whole time but you also don't want to pace back and forth too much. The solution is to move with a purpose. Transitions are generally a good time to make a move. Pause, take a few steps to the side, and reposition yourself as you transition from one point to another. Move in toward the audience when you want to drive home a key point. Then pause and move back a few steps to let it settle. If you're constantly pacing back and forth, work on planting yourself in one spot for a while before you take off again. Make a special notation in your notes about where and when to move. Look for transitions in your material and places where you want to hit your big points.

Facial Expressions: Get Your Face to Match Your Words

Picture this: a senior HR executive talking on video about how his firm was hiring nine thousand new people at a time when most other firms were experiencing layoffs. Clearly this was very positive news, yet if you looked at him as he spoke, his face was extremely serious, almost solemn. In other words, his face didn't match his message. As I was watching the tape, I decided to experiment. So I turned off the volume on my TV and just observed his body language. Sure enough, it looked as though he was saying that his firm was *laying off* nine thousand people, not hiring them. Talk about sending a mixed message! Yet in the business arena, this is an all too real, all too common problem. As soon as we step into the office we put on our serious masks whenever we speak. And more often than not, it sends the wrong visual image for our messages.

Furrowed brows and stern expressions can create the impression that you're overly concerned, worried, or unenthused about what you're saying. If you have good news to deliver, make sure you show it! Be expressive; break into a smile. An upbeat message requires you to wear an upbeat expression.

Eye Contact: It's About Connecting

Looking eyeball to eyeball is essential to building rapport with your audience. Unfortunately, many speakers make more eye contact with their presentation books or notes than they do with their audiences. Many don't maintain eye contact long enough with their audiences. This erodes credibility and trust. The same can be said for introductory handshakes. I've seen many presenters look away while they're still shaking hands at the start of a meeting. This breaks that critical first connection prematurely and creates a bad first impression.

How long should you look someone in the eye? Long enough to deliver a full thought or a piece of a thought. If you find yourself catching the faces of four or five people as you say one sentence, then you aren't spending enough time with each pair of eyes. When speaking to larger groups, the same rule applies. Don't just scan your audience or look at the back wall. Find a pair of eyes you can connect with and deliver your thought. Zero in on different faces as you move from thought to thought. The advantage of speaking to large groups is when you target a particular pair of eyes those who are sitting around that person will feel you're looking directly at them, too.

Also, don't fall into the habit of looking down at your notes before you've completed your thought. You don't want to break the connection with your audience just as you're saying something important. Finish your thought with your eyes on your listeners, take a second to glance down at your notes, and come up again. Take advantage of the natural break point that occurs whenever you complete a sentence. All you need is a split second to grab your next thought while your audience is absorbing what you just said.

One final tip: Observe the body language of professional spokespeople on television. Watch how they move and gesture. Look how they use and rest their hands. Notice their subtle head gestures. See how their facial expressions match their words. Take the good habits you observe and make them part of your own natural body language.

HOW TO SAY IT

1. Realize that your voice is a powerful communication tool and that how you use it determines how others respond to you.
2. Rid your voice of any unpleasant or irritating characteristics.
3. Add power and authority to your voice with simple exercises.
4. Speak with a rich, resonant voice at work.
5. Use your voice correctly to avoid straining it.
6. Avoid irritants that can harm your voice.
7. Stand and sit up straight, position your feet so your body is well balanced and open, and relax your shoulders.

8. Use big and broad gestures as you speak.
9. Move with a purpose.
10. Get your face to match your words.
11. Maintain eye contact with a listener long enough to deliver a full thought or piece of a thought.

HOW NOT TO SAY IT

1. Don't take your voice for granted.
2. Don't speak with an annoying voice.
3. Don't think you can't change the way you sound.
4. Don't strain your voice by forcing or shouting.
5. Don't lean back in your chair, hunch over, hide your hands, slouch, or swivel.
6. Don't forget about your posture when talking on the telephone.
7. Don't restrict yourself by thinking that you must keep your hands down or at your sides as you speak.
8. Don't pace back and forth.
9. Don't look too serious too much of the time.
10. Don't dart your eyes or scan your audience.

Conclusion

We've covered a lot of ground in this book. If you'll recall from the introduction I said that making a persuasive presentation requires a much broader set of skills than most people realize. You should now have a clear understanding of what it takes. Whether you interact in small, informal settings or talk to larger audiences, whether you're on the phone, on a panel, or behind a podium, you now have the tips and techniques to help you master any type of speaking situation.

As you progress, you'll become more aware of your own unique talents and learn how to make the most of them. This in turn will give you greater confidence to express yourself naturally, with authority and conviction, and allow you to perform at a higher level. And there's always another level to reach. It really depends on how far you want to go. It is my hope that you will have the desire and determination to develop your skills to their fullest potential and not be satisfied with meeting only the minimum standards. After all, the more skillful you are, the more options open up for you.

Remember, whether it's fair or not, you are judged by

the way you present yourself. And, ultimately, you are paid for the way you present yourself. There really is a bottom-line connection here. The greater your ability, the greater your earning potential. That's why improving your presentation skills is one of the best investments you'll ever make.

I believe this book will give you the foundation and impetus to get the job done. Use it well and reap the rewards!

About the Author

Jeffrey Jacobi has been helping people from every walk of life to improve their presentation performance for more than twenty years. Using a unique and practical approach, he counsels clients in government, media, law, and business, including many top executives from Fortune 500 companies, such as AT&T, American Express, Citigroup, DuPont, General Electric, Merrill Lynch, and Deutsche Bank. Jeff's expertise encompasses every facet of public speaking, including presentation skills, assertive speaking, accent-reduction training, voice and diction improvement, and on-air media training. Founder and President of Jacobi Persuasive Speaking in New York City, he is the author of *How to Say It: Persuasive Presentations* (Prentice Hall 2006), *How to Say It with Your Voice* (Prentice Hall 2000), *The Vocal Advantage* (Prentice Hall 1996), and *The Executive Voice Trainer* (Prentice Hall 1990). He has also taught speech communication at New York University. Jeff's innovative coaching methods have been featured in the *Wall Street Journal*, *New York Times*, *Los Angeles Times*, *USA Today*, *Businessweek*, and many other leading business and trade publications in the United States and abroad. He has appeared on a variety of radio and television programs, and holds both his bachelor's and master's degrees from the Juilliard School. In addition to his individual clients, he conducts problem-solving workshops and seminars for major corporations and other organizations.

For more information, contact:

JACOBI PERSUASIVE SPEAKING
New York City
212.787.6721
www.JacobiPersuasiveSpeaking.com